Dee Callahan

grace

IN THE FIRST PERSON

grace IN THE FIRST PERSON

Growing into Life and Faith

Lee Pearson Knapp

Fleming H. Revell
A Division of Baker Book House Co
Grand Rapids, Michigan 49516

© 2003 by Lee Pearson Knapp

Published by Fleming H. Revell
a division of Baker Book House Company
P.O. Box 6287, Grand Rapids, MI 49516-6287
www.bakerbooks.com

Printed in the United States of America

Library of Congress Cataloging-in-Publication Data
Knapp, Lee Pearson
        Grace in the first person : growing into life and faith / Lee Pearson
    Knapp.
            p.   cm.
        ISBN 0-8007-5813-7 (pbk.)
        1. Knapp, Lee Pearson. 2. Virginia—Biography. 3. Christian biog-
    raphy—Virginia. I. Title.
    CT275.K65 A3 2003
    975.5′04′092—dc21   2002014974

contents

Contents

Grace through the Daily Grind

introduction

About a fourth of the way into writing the first draft of this book, I found my voice. This was a much better proportion than the 50 percent of my life I have spent trying to figure out who I am. Since about the onset of adolescence, a healthy self-knowledge has floated in and out of my head like the Russian voices I used to hear on my father's Ham radio. The other half of the time I've tripped into the traps of comparing myself either to someone else or to some impossible standard. Once my voice emerged on paper loudly enough for me to recognize it as being mine, a couple of points kept recurring. I have labored a long time and in many realms to manufacture an identity, a sort of composite of what I admired in others and what the culture told me was appealing. No wonder a stubborn, low-grade dissatisfaction crept into my soul. In some of the other stories, the voice led me to see that the best way to combat my cravings for some imagined self and lifestyle is to revel in the joy, humor, and even ridiculousness of the small moments of my very real life. Whether they concern wrestling with (and losing) the have-and-do-it-all men-

7

tality of my generation, coming to appreciate the brilliant clown who was my father, or taking lessons on life from my dog, these stories have been therapeutic.

I have realized that the purpose for self-discovery, the answer to that ubiquitous call of our society to "just be yourself," might be more than simply to provide a salve for my own psychological and emotional scrapes. Perhaps there is a connection between accepting myself as God has designed me and making some kind of contribution to his creation. The link may have something to do with true freedom. Those bear traps of insecurity that lie around, not all that well camouflaged, in this world not only cost me important parts of myself, but keep me from moving forward and being of real use to those around me.

I suppose this book could fall loosely into the genre of memoir, but the random nature of the narratives makes that a stretch. Memoir connotes chronological order, an organized history of one's experiences. That's going to be difficult for me. Rather than momentous dates, I tend to recall little turning points, small infusions of grace "in the first person" that spun the dimmer switch of my soul around to make it a bit brighter.

By far, the greatest evidences of grace, wholly unexpected and full of love, are the second, third, fourth, and fifth persons in my life. I want to dedicate this book to them. My three sons, Cheston, Eric, and Stephen—who by the way have each waived their right to sue for slander—stand simply as miracles to me, never ceasing to amaze. My husband, Fritz, thankfully didn't answer, "Friends," when I shocked him long ago with the question, "So . . . how *would* you classify our relationship?" After twenty-three years of marriage, he is my greatest love and my best friend.

grace
FROM MY DNA

late bloomers

> He has made everything beautiful in its time.
>
> Ecclesiastes 3:11 NIV

Just about every February the weather warms up for a couple of days and a few yellow crocuses shoot out of the ground around my lamppost. If they bloomed in the spring with all the other underachieving buds I might be able to see them for what they really are, but on the gray landscape the flowers strike me as more odd than pretty. But for these few short days the tiny yellow cups have the corner on the nature market before the returning cold of winter marks them for an early death.

February also marks approximately the midpoint of a seemingly endless basketball season at the YMCA. When my middle son Eric was in the seventh grade, he played in a league that combined seventh, eighth, and ninth graders. Nature's staggered blooming showed up in that gymnasium full of boys too. Eric had not grown as tall as many of his peers, and the "short" complex sent him face down into his pillow plenty of times that year. To make matters worse, it was common for well-meaning old ladies in the grocery store to mistake him for the twin of his brother Stephen, who was a full three years younger. At twelve, Eric was sure he would be in the circus one day.

One Saturday of that season, Eric's red-jerseyed team played the blue team. Starting at their feet, these guys were big. Their legs were hairy, their calf muscles were well defined, and their biceps bulged when they took their warm-up shots. Most wore tank tops, not T-shirts, which showed off the ultimate sign of early manhood—armpit hair. That week's game was refereed by James, a Danny Glover look-alike who wore a steady grin that threatened to break into a full-bore guffaw given the slightest excuse, of which there were many when motley middle schoolers took to the court. Before each game, as was the YMCA's policy, the referee said a prayer as both teams and the coaches huddled around him. Except for a few glimpses of red jerseys, it was hard to spot our team in that circle. James prayed a perfunctory prayer for sportsmanship, but I'm pretty sure our guys were adding a few supplications of their own having to do with valleys of evil and their opponents' five o'clock shadows of death.

Once James blew the whistle, the Jolly Blue Giants ran up and down the court so often, the spectators looked like we were at a tennis match. Our guys trotted along behind the blue players and did a lot of wincing and leaning away if they happened to catch up with the blue team under the basket. The red team did play good defense—it was just self-defense. Eric employed never-before-tried basketball techniques that would have made James Naismith blow his whistle from the grave—

moves like "shirt grabbing" and "hanging over the back of one's opponent," especially common with one player we nicknamed Jethro. This hulk fee-fie-foe-fummed up and down the court, never noticing he had two or three red, numbered mosquitoes stuck to the back of his uniform. Eric finally resorted to making faces at the "boy" to distract him rather than actually trying to steal the ball away from him. At the end of the game we learned that this kid was not a twenty-seven-year-old ninth grader but, like my "vertically challenged" son, was only in the seventh grade.

My in-laws had come to that game with us. Their thirty-plus years of experience raising five boys came in handy while we all witnessed this pituitary injustice. They reminded me that their middle boy, my six-foot-one brother-in-law Andy, was still only about five and a half feet tall in his junior year of high school. Chet, the second in line, wrestled 98 pounds his junior year and 125 his senior year but by the beginning of his sophomore year in college weighed 180. The youngest, Chris, was often mistaken in the eleventh grade as a twelve- or thirteen-year-old. In fact, none of the boys hit six feet until college, except the oldest, my husband Fritz, who stopped growing a couple of inches short of that mark, which undoubtedly gave the oft-punched younger brothers a sense of divine justice.

This late-bloomer gene was no consolation for Eric, because to him, like to all twelve-year-olds, it seemed he would be in middle school for the rest of his life. Not only during basketball games but at many other times in his adolescence he would become irate at his disadvantage and make the jump that most of us do when we feel overpowered, claiming that life has been specifically unfair to him—the belief that everyone else is perfect, but nature picked out *me* to showcase in its index under "Freak of." I tried to comfort my enraged son by

13

saying that his height had nothing to do with fairness and everything to do with timing. In due time, he too would grow. Being a late bloomer requires a lot of patience and a strong sense of who you are on the inside, despite the fact that in high school you still shop in the little boys' department.

Yet my comforting remarks may have come less from my motherhood credentials and more from my own deep psychological recesses where an insecure, pimpled adolescent me still lurked, trying to put me in that "freak" index too. Eric would grow. His height would be measurable on the doorjamb in the dining room. I, however, was already full to overgrown and shouldn't have been struggling with my own seemingly retarded flowering process any longer.

As plainly as the natural order all around me demonstrates that it is impossible, I have wanted the desires of my heart and the toil of my hands to produce instant results, like the time-lapsed National Geographic films of lilies blooming or baby chicks hatching. Anything I could imagine producing—whether it was art or money or children—would seamlessly and gracefully unfold while a soft-spoken narrator gently explained every well-ordered and beautiful phase. But in my experience, life hasn't work that way. My goals have sputtered out, like water from a knotted-up garden hose.

When my Big Zero year was approaching, I was defending myself against the feeling that zero was also the sum total of my life. I couldn't get the thought out of my mind that by forty I should be slam-dunking life in a tank top with armpits full of hair too. Like Eric's, my desire for stature and my need to achieve something really big by then had grown so overblown that it blurred a long-ago strongly held sense of identity. I should have heeded my own advice to Eric, only slightly adjusted for middle age: You do need a deep sense of who you are on the inside when surrounded, seemingly, by people whose glands drained way before yours.

I know this sense of coming up short is natural when faced with big milestones in life. My life was good when measured by realistic standards and timeless values, so what caused the hum of healthy self-awareness to turn into a sonic boom of inferiority? It probably had something to do with the frenetic and grotesquely ambitious eighties and nineties, when it was impossible to avoid *Lifestyles of the Rich and Famous.* My ego fell into the trap of wanting to be famous too, to join that never-ending party in the television. Never mind that the most famous people in our society got that way by pretending to be someone else on a screen; they were beautiful but artificial flowers. Perhaps the hot climate of those years brought out in me an onus of achievement and its ugly sister, the need to impress, a need stemming from having my moment in the sun in February, way too early to matter.

High school, which began right after sixth grade back in my day, started out a little rough. Unlike Eric's, my big seventh grade struggle was not with being little; it was with bone structure. Not basketball but cheerleading tryouts made my weaknesses painfully clear. Besides the fact that cheerleaders do a lot of springy things with their bodies, I should have known it was not going to be my gig. I was much more serious than peppy as a kid. At the ripe old age of seven, I told my great-aunt in response to her asking me how I liked second grade, "This has been the hardest year of my life." That assessment held through middle school until tenth grade, when I finally got what I had been looking for—acceptance and a place in the school culture. Joining clubs, running for offices, and getting good grades were my drugs of choice in the seventies.

15

The résumé I amassed in high school culminated in my senior class voting me "Most Likely to Succeed." Looking back now, I think that while flattering, this title was actually rather cruel. If you're voted Wittiest, you get a certain social confidence that lasts a lifetime. Being chosen Friendliest is a great thing to tell your kids about yourself. But Most Likely to Succeed carries a burden of proof that is missed at eighteen, but painfully obvious at forty. It would have been easier to be voted Least Likely to Succeed. I think my classmates gave me that title since there wasn't a category for "Biggest Goody-Goody."

As it turned out, I actually did succeed in life, specifically in the area of creating it. A completely unexpected thing happened to me in college: I met a boy. We fell madly in love, got married, and both became teachers. Two years later we were parents. Eighteen months after that we were a family of four. My mother said that pretty soon we'd figure out what was causing these babies, but we didn't before our third boy was born, two and one-half years later.

For those first few years of my marriage, the very early eighties, big numbers had not yet created benchmarks for our self-worth. The stock market hadn't even broken a thousand, but it wasn't long before Michael Douglas uttered the movie line that summed up the decade: "Greed is good." The power decade had begun in earnest—pink ties, fern bars, working women who didn't need to clarify "outside the home" yet. What self-respecting, college-educated female wouldn't be working outside the home?

Me. I was very much inside the home on a perpetual pacifier hunt that often led me at midnight into the back-yard with a flashlight to find the tooth-pitted rubber nipple. When not searching for the binky, I was cutting up hot dogs and trying to get that nasal passage–clearing baby wipe smell off my hands. Instead of climbing the corporate ladder, I was climbing the walls. The only deals I followed were on diapers at Toys "R" Us. Whenever I did have a chance to read anything other than *Go, Dog. Go!* ("Do you like my hat?"), I tried to avoid the alumni newspaper after seeing one too many of my college classmates' names screaming at me with important sounding titles next to them. They probably had been voted Most Likely to Succeed by their high schools too, and there they were, doing it in bold ink. They were ultimate eighties, falling nicely into their newfound acronymic identities of yuppies and dinks. Meanwhile, I spent my days in our dinky rental house, sitting on the sofa at 3:30 in the afternoon eating animal crackers out of a little circus box, listening to Big Bird tell me in his grating voice, "You can be anything you dream of."

Who was I anymore? A couple of simpatico friends and I often met very late at our neighborhood Friendly's restaurant for coffee during those years to answer that question for each other. We would stay until one o'clock in the morning, then keep talking even later in one of our driveways to reassure each other of our worth among the land mines of the day. Explosions of self-esteem were common on the landscape of phrases like "working mother," the ever-depressing "just a mother," and the most dreaded, "Do you work?" My friend Dianne was at a college homecoming football game early on in "real life" when someone she barely knew from college days sat next to her in the bleachers. Trying to make conversation, he asked a question that landed on her like an anvil on Wile E. Coyote, "So what do you do?" She thought a moment, then decided to answer the oxford shirt, blue blazer boy in a decidedly truthful way. "Well, I've been reading a lot of books, contemplating the meaning of life, and scraping cheese off linoleum with my fingernails." He nodded politely before turning to the person to his left and cheering on our team. Dianne said it was worth every bit of the awkwardness.

If history makes men, it had undone me in those years. But from where I sit now, the view has changed. I see that the past couple of decades have been as freakish as the crocuses around my lamppost. When did twenty-five-year-olds start expecting to own their own companies and have a million dollars in the bank? Only people don't keep money in banks anymore, I've heard. The success stories that burst on the scene early got a lot of attention, but they are still an oddity. It is much more natural to be young and poor and happy. Life will come along at its own pace, not be forced out like an amaryllis bulb at Christmastime. In the early years of raising our kids, it was difficult to believe that, though.

I know a little more about process now, which helps put blooming in perspective. For instance, those National Geographic time-lapsed films don't show the long periods of fallow time required for productivity. Once I got out of my thirties, that perverse need to prove something to the world began eroding, and it is being replaced by a growing desire simply to create something beautiful and lasting out of whatever pile of fertilizer lands on me. Though I am in no way a farmer, I do know that what comes out of seeded fields of manure is known as its yield. Perhaps it's no accident that yielding is also a state of mind, one that did not come naturally in my youth. What has really been freaky, though, is that contrary to conventional wisdom, I'm noticing that this old acreage yields a lot more life than it did twenty years ago. All that inner turmoil to nervously make something of myself didn't yield anything worth picking at all back then.

I look back with some sadness to see that the whole time my generation of women was causing each other to feel either guilty or worthless, little kids were growing up. Whenever an old lady, usually the same ones who insulted Eric's ego, said to me in the grocery store, "Enjoy them now, they grow so fast," I would smile politely, all the while thinking, "Are you kidding? Each day seems like an eternity." Right about then one of the boys, who insisted on pushing the cart, would slam it into the back of my ankles just to prove my point. The old ladies were right, though, and what's worse, I'm quickly becoming one of them, an old lady who smiles at young mothers wrestling candy out of their children's hands in the checkout line. They think I'm smiling at the cute kids. I'm really privately thanking God that it's them and not me.

But sure enough, the most important achievements in my life, the ones that didn't require a lot of education or training, other than on-the-job, are fast becoming men. The seeds of my fret-filled youth are blossoming at breakneck speed, and they are beautiful. Eric is approaching six feet and is now even taller than his father. For my middle son and me, what seemed so urgent and intensely important a few years ago—being big—is very difficult to recall now. Both of us worried too much about what was in store instead of trusting that nature would take its course. In any kind of growing, physical or spiritual, I'm afraid there is no other choice.

the great one

For now we see in a mirror dimly, but then face to face.

1 Corinthians 13:12

It wouldn't be right to say my father had a few idiosyncrasies. He was an idiosyncrasy. For starters, Daddy bore an unusual birthmark over his left ear that looked like a dollop of tapioca pudding, tiny fleshy bumps about the size of a quarter. As a little girl, I used to poke at this soft spot on his head, and he'd feign, "Doh, stop, that hurts!" and tell me it was a scar from the war in Germany. He'd describe how a bullet came right for him and he froze in his tracks just as it grazed his head in the space between his ear and his G. I. Joe helmet. I believed him every single time before remembering the truth. I'd tease back, "Nuh uh, nobody ever shot at you!" then run to the den in time to see Tinkerbell light up *The Wonderful World of Disney*.

Daddy reminded me a lot of Jackie Gleason with his square head and beautiful wavy black hair. He had the same girth as the Great One too, which came in handy when my brothers and I were very little. After work, he'd stretch out on his back in the living room with his eyes closed and let us jump up and down on his big round stomach, laughing and laughing, until dinner was ready. Daddy liked this low-effort fun, especially since by then he had already passed forty. From his Russian-born mother, Daddy had inherited a distinctive facial trait— matching Samsonite train cases hanging under his eyes, so puffy it seemed a needle would pop them like blisters.

My parents married at what was considered a late age in their era and were a full decade older than most of my friends' parents, so by the time I entered middle school my father's wavy black hair had become much more salt than pepper. His front-loaded body would have given any tailor the challenge of a career—that is, if Daddy didn't already get his clothes from one of those Pennsylvania mail-order places. He was a sucker for their slick Sunday paper inserts, which advertised four different shades of pants—made of an early type of polyester spun from recycled bicycle inner tubes—for one low price. In the '70s he even ventured into their leisure suit line and very well might have been their only customer. The powder blue model with a Nehru collar was his favorite, even into the preppy '80s, but he gave up the khaki bellboy-style one with a stand-up collar, red satin–lined cuffs, and gold buttons when a man in a store asked him if he was the security guard. By then his weight was down, but he still had a big barrel belly and a rear end as flat as a piece of plywood. This lopsided body profile was propped up on two stick-thin legs that rarely saw the light of day.

Daddy's lack of "hip" became public knowledge one bright Saturday afternoon of my seventh grade year. He took me to a nearby strip mall so I could spend my babysitting money on a Monkees album I'd seen at People's Drug Store. When I was in first and second grades, Daddy and I often went to People's to get a Cherry Smash and a box of Panatelas. We'd sit in a booth—me drinking my Coke with maraschino cherry juice, him smoking a cigar—and just talk silliness. That may have been when I first realized that my father was nothing if not a prolific talker. He tickled me with words like "slopjaw" and "slushpump" and mimicked my childish pronunciations of phrases like "glabben club," as in "Mumma grows flowers in the glabben club." He loved to call me "doll baby" and my brothers "whistle britches," but that was well before I fell under the spell of Davy, Mickey, Peter, and Michael. Not only were these Monkees cute and funny on their TV show, they tapped into my growing sense of social justice when they sang right to me about the power of monkeying around, challenging me to be "too busy singing to put anybody down."

Walking out of the drugstore on that sunny Saturday, I stared longingly at the four Monkee faces on the album cover. I couldn't wait to get home to listen to those prophetic lyrics about how we were "the new generation and we've got something to say." What I didn't know was that the old generation was about to render me speechless. Daddy had walked on ahead, and I watched him step off the sidewalk and head into the parking lot. He was approaching the back of our blue Pontiac when it happened: a moment that would forever set my dad miles apart from most other—no, all other—fathers I knew.

As though they had been yanked, Daddy's mail-order pants dropped straight to his ankles. And I dropped like a meteor behind the blue U.S. mailbox fastened to the sidewalk, hoping no one I knew had seen me with him. I peered out from the side of the mailbox to see my dad's spindly, white legs gleaming in the sunlight, shooting out from a pool of green, 100 percent genuine polyester like toothpicks in olives on an hors d'oeuvres tray. His barrel belly stood exposed to the open air, and to my ears it seemed to be screaming at passersby to check out its pink-patterned boxer shorts. Still crouching behind my cover, looking like Stymie when he's in a jam, I watched as my dad calmly and deliberately bent down, grabbed his trousers off the asphalt, and unbuckled and rebuckled the useless belt around the area of his torso that could have been loosely called his waist. He acted like this was a common occurrence, which, sadly, it would become. But I felt no nonchalance. As a junior high kid with more than my share of self-consciousness, I glanced quickly to my left and to my right. Once I felt enough time had passed to disassociate me from my father, I ran a zigzag pattern through W. T. Grant & Co.'s parking lot like a soldier running through a field surrounded by snipers.

That *sans culottes* episode happened when I was about thirteen. When Daddy was thirteen, his father had a heart attack and died alone in the dark during a Sunday matinee. It was the height of the Great Depression, so my father immediately got a job at the A&P earning 25 cents a week filling old ladies' grocery orders by gathering the items from the back of the store and bringing them to the front counter. He saved his money to buy himself a treat once a month during those hard times. I can imagine him sneaking into a darkened back room of his mother's boarding house on a Saturday night to savor the Coca-Cola and cookie he'd been eyeing for weeks at the A&P. Later he worked at an auto parts store, even after he graduated from high school in June 1941. Then, just three weeks shy of his eighteenth birthday that same year, Pearl Harbor was attacked. My father rushed to enlist in the Army.

For my entire childhood, and even now at times, picturing my father at war was a true test of my imagination. Nothing of what I knew of him, especially his bouts
with pantlessness, could be reconciled with saving Western civilization from Hitler. Daddy himself portrayed
the war more often in terms of a fraternity party than
an armed conflict with an evil despot. He'd talk about
washing his socks in his helmet or setting the latrine on
fire or laugh about the night he was walking an empty
street and met an unarmed German who threw his
hands up and yelled, "Nicht schiessen, nicht schiessen!"
He told, with no addendum about wartime ethics, about
a buddy from Long Island who stole a German's motorcycle by pushing it out of a town they captured. At the
dinner table, he was fond of speaking pseudo-German
with phrases like, "Passun meun da salten."

One night when I was seventeen, the same age he was
when he went off to war, I wanted to prove to myself
that he actually had been part of the great, defining
struggle of the twentieth century that I had just studied
in my high school history class. With the tact of a self-
important, new generation teenager, I flatly asked him
if he'd ever shot anyone. Now I had hit the real soft spot
in his head. He wouldn't look at me. After a few seconds
of a rare and uncomfortable silence, I got up from the
table and went into the den to see if Gilligan just might
get off that uncharted desert isle that week. Daddy never
did answer me.

As silly as he was about almost everything else, things
and their upkeep were no laughing matter, an attitude
probably going back to that monthly cookie of his childhood. I spent many a night out in the driveway of our
1950s ranch tract house, leaning against an American-
made beauty like the Bel-Air, the Vista-Cruiser, the
Safari, or his favorite, the Bonneville, holding the light
for him as he worked. It was so boring just standing

there with my arm going numb while he narrated every step of his operation. With inanimate objects like cars he had superhuman patience, but that patience evaporated if he found the top off the milk or one of his tools in the yard.

It did not take me long to figure out that my dad would never be a *Father Knows Best* dad who bounced me on his knee dispensing words of wisdom. If he had watched TV he would have called that show "sappy." Even though I knew it deeply, I cannot remember him saying outright that he loved me. But when it came to using his mechanical mind and that patience to help me fix or assemble something, he was better than Robert Young or Ward Cleaver, with their thin ties and sporty suits that I bet never once fell off in a parking lot, ever could have been. Maybe helping was Daddy's way of showing the love he was uncomfortable expressing with words. But even that line of thinking would have been "psychological garbage" to him. He got involved with our projects not consciously out of love for us but because they represented an intellectual challenge.

When I bought my first car, a ten-year-old '65 Volkswagen, he went into tirades about the inevitable astronomical repair costs and came close to questioning my patriotism. But when I couldn't get the front seats off their greasy tracks to reupholster them, he came outside to help me under the porch light one late June night. Together we squeezed on those Sears' Naugahyde seat covers like Mammy lacing up Scarlett O'Hara's corset. When all the cussing and sweating was over, Daddy went inside and left me to do the easier bench seat myself. My old VW still looked like an old VW, but now it had white fake leather upholstery that I had done myself with his help. Looking back, those were the times I felt the most love from, and the most like, my father.

Because my dad had worked in an auto parts store before the war, when he returned from Germany he applied for a job selling auto parts. It saddens me still to think that his brilliance in electronics and physics was relegated to his hobbies. (He built an oscilloscope in his bedroom one summer—I guess because he needed to get a real good look at some oscilloes up close.) Despite the encouragement he'd received, something in his personality—perhaps a general pessimism brought on by his father's early death or by seeing so many young men killed in the war—created a greater need for security than for self-fulfillment. Maybe he never explored how he could get paid for using his brain because he lacked confidence in himself and had no role model. But these are my assumptions, coming from a very different time in history when risks are always good and mastering life is like getting at those smoked oysters Daddy loved mixed with mustard on a cracker—you just have to pull the key off the bottom of the can and open it up. For whatever reason, my father wasn't wired to take risks and became a traveling auto parts salesman whose customers often ordered things they didn't really need just so he would stop talking.

Like Willy Loman, Daddy saw it all as a salesman. He'd been laid off, had his territory cut back, and was generally jerked around in all his jobs, and he just took it. Then he had the opportunity to buy his own small auto parts company. This petrified him, but my mother urged, or rather pushed, him to do it because she knew he was smart and needed to gain some control over his future. For the first ten months after taking the plunge and buying Auto Electric Parts Company, that was easier said than done. He became overwhelmed with fear, sank into a deep depression, and started drinking every night. I'd often walk in from some high school meeting and follow the snoring sound to find him passed out on the couch. Daddy drifted away so much that he didn't even want to talk on his ham radio like I'd seen him do my whole life. (He'd hold the Johnny Carson–type microphone close to his lips and say, "This is K4MKK. Come in Russia, come in Russia." Before long I'd hear that Russian accent saying—repeatedly during my dad's chatter—something like, "OK USA, Dasvadanya K4MKK, Dasvadanya.") I learned later his depression wasn't caused by the incurred debt but by an inherited employee who was siphoning off money from the company. When he finally got up his nerve to fire the guy, my father was a completely new man. The morning of his moment of truth, Daddy was depressed and incommunicado; that night he was giddy and bright-eyed, telling us over and over again about the look of shock on the poor guy's face.

Auto Electric stood at the end of a half block of row houses that had been converted to businesses in a run-down section of Richmond's main drag, Broad Street. The bottom floor had a plate glass window and an old creaky door with AUTO ELECTRIC PARTS COMPANY painted in gold in a circle on its large window. One side of the store lined an alley that separated it from the post office. Down that long, windowless, two-story brick wall was painted the gigantic logo of ACDelco Parts in red, white, and blue. Whenever my mother and I went shopping downtown, I looked for that logo, and once I spotted it I would think, "My Dad's in there. He's the boss." In the summers of my early teen years he was my boss too. Each summer day, Daddy and I would ride "down to the store" together in his Pontiac. We walked in that old plate glass door to the hum of the huge air conditioner, he in his short sleeved shirt and rubber knit pants, me with my stringy hair parted in the middle and my little sleeveless dress. We greeted the employees every morning like we were the king and his princess.

27

My job was to help the widow bookkeeper, Mrs. Utley, upstairs, an area of utter filth and clutter except for the fabulously air-conditioned office. I filed pink, carbon-drenched copies of invoices into tight folders marked "Hill and Dale Auto," "Heater Hose Heaven," or "Manny's Transmission Service" between trips down and under the stairwell to get a little Coke out of the old-time red machine. I remember noticing, during the summer around eighth grade, one of the employees who seemed to be particularly misfit there. Andy, whose father also worked at the store, was a cute, preppy-looking guy in his late twenties who always wore button-collared shirts. He spent a lot of time just sitting at the parts counter, silent. Whenever I emerged from the oily, black aisles of tall shelves of auto parts after using the restroom downstairs, I'd see him from the back, sitting on a metal stool, staring out the big window at the parking lot of the Super Fresh. The sight of Andy Campbell on that stool, staring away his twenties, may have been the seed of my budding existentialism. Everything about his body language cried, "Why am I here? What is the point?"

The cast of characters at Auto Electric fluctuated over the years, but all of them, while never able to fully understand or relate to him, got a kick out of my father. They marveled at how he calculated tax and did long division in his head and even more at his prolific "flapjaw," as he himself would have termed it. I often heard the employees laughing about how Daddy, in a complete role reversal, talked a drop-in saleman right out of the store with detailed banter about the history of the fan belt and the nuances of thermostats. He was particulary fluent in the finer points of the voltage regulator, having rebuilt dozens of them for extra income in his work cubby at home.

This back room office, a kind of upstairs dungeon, stood at the rear of the house down a narrow gold hallway lined with family photos, some sepia-toned, some black-and-white. Daddy installed shelving all the way to the ceiling in there to hold what could be called his "hobbyabilia"—gadgets, stamp collections, and slide carousels and home movie cans cataloged by year. When my brothers and I were little, we'd open our mouths in amazement at the clever "opening credits" he'd added, funny signs that disappeared in a shrinking black circle.

Somewhere in those stacks of films was my favorite: Mom and Daddy at the Cavalier Beach Club in Virginia Beach when they were dating. The women had tight perms and big skirts and most of the men had fifths of whiskey in their pockets. But not my future father. In the black-and-white silence, as Sarah and Ed twirl around the dance floor, you see a debonair Daddy with a Radio Institute manual folded in half in his back pocket. Thirty years later, plenty more manuals lined the shelves in his upstairs room, with coordinating certificates of completion hanging on what free wall space remained. He was most definitely a person known by his things.

Nearing the end of the seventies, it was getting to be Daddy's turn to be the president of his men's group. Despite the fact that he had known these people for over twenty years, he grew more and more debilitated by anxiety at the prospect of being up front and in charge. When he and my mother came to see me at college to celebrate my twenty-first birthday, his face just drooped with sadness. In the restaurant he confessed to me an inferiority complex he'd been fighting his whole life. This would have been too much to bear if he had been the typical father. It pained me to see him so pained, but I never thought less of him—this was Daddy. I encouraged him to have faith that night, and wrote in my journal at the time that the conversation was "neet."

As the economy's recession deepened during those same years, so did my father's depression. Being the captain of a quickly sinking ship full of auto parts brought it on full bore, and this bout lasted five years. He spent more and more of his time on the couch and less and less at Auto Electric, and he resumed his familiar pattern of drinking himself to sleep each night around 8:30, then denying it the next day. I had to watch my mother mark the bottles of scotch and then confront his lies with her proof. Needless to say, the atmosphere in the house was tense. I tried to encourage him during that dark time by making a Magic Markered calligraphy picture of Proverbs 3:5–6. With green ivy vines winding around the first letter of each line, my little gift read, "Trust in the Lord with all your heart, / Lean not unto your own understanding. / In all your ways acknowledge him, / And He will make straight your paths."

But times would be bad and paths still crooked for Daddy for a long while, even though he put on a good face to walk me down the grass aisle at my outdoor wedding. Because of Daddy's looks, the minister wondered to my mother if my father had a drink before the 4:00 ceremony. I really wasn't aware of anything odd, except that he seemed quiet and a little puffy in the face. But by the time they came to visit my new husband Fritz and me at our honeymoon summer job on Martha's Vineyard, he seemed dazed with sadness, and my mother was at her wit's end. They were a far cry from the New England, outdoorsy types anyway, but nothing we did could lift the tension and the mood. My dad even complained about how odd his eggs tasted and that his swordfish had an unappetizing sour flavor. They all tasted fine to us, and the "bad swordfish" became a little joke.

He ended up in the hospital, diagnosed with Crohn's disease, which made us feel terrible for belittling his complaints. It wasn't life threatening but it was uncomfortable, especially since he couldn't drink. Actually Daddy seemed relieved to be sick so he could get away from Auto Electric since his heart was just not in it anymore. His face had turned a pinkish color and looked older than its fifty-eight years. Even though it hurt to see him so sick, we became more and more exasperated with his endless supply of self-pity and sadness. He was trapped in a double bind of circumstances and natural pessimism and didn't see—or seem to want to see—a way out. That was before he had an encounter in the hospital bathroom.

My father always was an early riser, and even in the hospital awoke at 5:30. One of those mornings near the end of his three-week stay, he shuffled to the bathroom in his pajamas and slippers and took a shower. In the steam-enveloped room he wrapped a towel around his waist, stood in front of the mirror, and prepared to shave. He clutched the sides of the sink with his thin arms, and his head hung down as he waited for the water to fill the sink. As he looked up in the mirror he saw through the steam a clear image of Christ standing behind him, silent. Daddy told me how, without any thought, he dropped straight to his knees and bowed his head in prayer at the little sink, the steam still swirling around him. In one of only two times I ever saw his eyes well with tears, he told me how he was speechless as a voice called him by name over and over and told him to trust.

I don't know if that bathroom vision says more about Jesus or my father. I do know that those days had been filled with despair and much conversation between my mother and me about Daddy's self-destruction, and suddenly because of this small but huge miracle, those talks ended. As with the other roles he'd found himself playing in life—soldier, family man, businessman—my

31

father was a most unlikely choice to be a visionary. I often wonder now if his complete lack of self-consciousness may have had a kind of upside, especially in spiritual matters. He truly accepted the truths of the Bible with childlike simplicity and committed his life to Christ every time the invitation was given, most often when my mother took him to Men's Night events of some of her women's groups. A couple of times they attended Bible studies, but the picture of my dad sitting in a circle having a discussion—with other people—unfolds in my mind like a Salvador Dali painting. He enjoyed church and Sunday school, and especially loved Palm Sunday when he joined a group of men to cook breakfast for everyone. But to study how to live, rather than actually pursue life, even though his life was mostly in his head, did not seem to have much of a point to him. His quirkiness ultimately didn't really matter, but I think his openness did. The truth is, to this day I am jealous of his vision and get more faith from it than from any wisdom he may have tried, uncharacteristically, to pass on. It endears me to God to remember that when my father was utterly hopeless, he saw himself in a mirror the way he always should have—with his Maker firmly behind him.

After the vision, Daddy's circumstances had not changed, but his depression immediately lifted and he stopped drinking all at once, the same way he had stopped smoking cigarettes at age thirty—just threw a pack off a bridge and never smoked them again. While Auto Electric's business did gradually improve, Daddy's mind was moving elsewhere, and he let my younger brother Brian, a business major in college by then, take on more and more of its responsibilities. Besides, Daddy had a new reason to live, and, true to his more earthly nature, it had nothing to do with his hospital vision. Despite being utterly faithful to my mother, he had found a new love, for a price, at a popular hangout called Radio Shack.

Like Norm on the TV show *Cheers,* my dad would walk into our local Radio Shack and all the pocket-protected salesmen would raise their hands and hail him with a simultaneous "Ed!" Even back when he was in the hospital he bored the nurses and fascinated the doctors with his TRS-80, a sort of Cro-Magnon PalmPilot, before moving up to Radio Shack's earliest desktop model. There was no such thing as Windows or any other operating system then, which was how he liked it. To justify the immense amount of time he was spending programming this primeval function machine, he said he was saving the company time and money with business applications like payroll and inventory control. None of us would have had any idea if he were telling the truth or not.

When I was a teacher, he sold me on letting him average my grades on his computer "in a fraction of the time." I drove out to my parents' house one night to witness this miraculous machine and instead got a lot of, "Okay. Wait a minute. I just have to . . . Hold on. Something is a little off . . ." I grabbed a pencil and paper and sat in their bedroom with my grade book. Forty-five minutes later I waltzed down the little hallway to his office where he sat in his boxer shorts, staring at a black monitor that blinked with little white slash marks, arrows, colons, and block letters. I fully expected to hear the screen say in alien, clothes-pinned-nose tones, "That does not compute. That does not compute." He looked up at me and before he could "explain," I said, "Done. Thanks anyway, Daddy," and left. He carried on, probably all night, trying to get the kinks out of the program.

By the time the nineties began, Daddy's other hobbies had become like old girlfriends when true love is found. Totally infatuated with the computer, Daddy whispered sweet nothings into the TRS's memory every morning, noon, and night. By then I was a grown woman, but I remember standing at the door to his room in the afternoon, looking at him in his threadbare boxers, his chicken legs crossed neatly under his stomach, and feeling the same way I did when I held the light for him as a kid. This time instead of explaining the inner workings of the car, he narrated every last detail of how he programmed this machine and what he knew it could do. If you were going to take the risk of going down that hall, you had to have an exit strategy, or be able to entertain yourself with thoughts of movies or grocery lists while he droned on. During some of those "discussions," I began to notice that behind the smell of coffee, a hint of smoke came through.

Daddy never would have been called the picture of health even before his Crohn's disease. At sixty-three he had quadruple bypass surgery after doctors discovered his arteries were dangerously clogged. Before he actually went under the knife, he didn't seem too worried, if acting any more ridiculously was any sign. Since my three boys weren't allowed in the hospital, we all stood outside Daddy's first floor hospital window in the grass. From his hospital bed, Daddy did a little pantomime for them, pretending to rip open his chest, reach into the cavity, pull out an imaginary beating heart while it pulsated in his hands, and then drop it on the floor in wide-eyed surprise. (The boys were used to him by then. When our oldest was six, as my dad was making goofy faces on the back porch and my mother was waving good-bye, he said in the car, "Mamaw's cute and Didi's weird. They should have kids.")

My father came through that surgery feeling great, but we would find out later that he'd ignored the doctor's orders about smoking cigars. To hide his habit, he'd sit up in his back room and blow the smoke out the window. True to his love of gadgets, he also bought a couple of "clean air machines" that my openly antitechnology mother could easily have thought were computers. Then, in the middle of his sixties, his voice began to sound funny, as though he always needed to clear his throat. Five years after his heart surgery, tiny nodes of cancer were growing on his vocal chords. In a matter of months he could speak only in a harsh whisper. No matter how often he'd had "diarrhea of the mouth," as my mother so lovingly described his condition, we all longed to hear his real voice again, but we never would.

The cancer soon spread to his lungs, and it was the worst kind. Daddy carried on in good spirits during the radiation treatments and summoned his strength to sit at his computer as often as he could that winter. He did tell Mom one day near their March 12th anniversary that he was afraid of not being around for Christmas, but that was the only mention he ever made of death. The last time I saw him at home he was in his familiar uniform—threadbare boxers and a T-shirt—sitting in his swivel chair with one of his big books open across his lap. In an unusually pensive mood and in a deep, painful whisper he told me how happy he was that my older brother was getting married soon. The next day the rescue squad had to come and abruptly take him from his back room to the emergency room because he couldn't breathe.

Many of his old auto parts buddies, neighbors, and folks from church came to see him in the hospital over the next few days. But one afternoon only my younger brother Brian and I were in the room with Daddy when a nurse came in. When she turned toward me to fix the sheets, Daddy started making faces to me behind her back. I didn't know whether to be heartened by this emergence of his old self, or even more saddened knowing it might be one of his last private performances. I hid my emotions and made pleasantries with the nurse, knowing full well Daddy was watching me to see if I'd laugh.

Brian, by then in his early thirties, had been virtually running Auto Electric for several years. He and Daddy shared a lot about the day-to-day operation of the business, but Daddy's mind had long been melded to the hard drive of his TRS-80. As my father lay flat in his hospital bed with a big tube coming out of his side to drain his lungs, my little brother crouched close to him under the fluorescent light to ask him some questions. Daddy answered them by scrawling something on a piece of paper or shaking his head yes or no. One glitch in the computer system that my father had programmed had been particularly stubborn over the past few nights. Brian finally figured out the right question to ask and got a couple of Pearson commands scribbled on an ACDelco notepad. Lots of visitors came later that night, and for the first time he looked very pained. I found myself getting angry that they were hanging around so long, perhaps because I sensed that this would be his last night. Finally they left, and not long afterwards he motioned for us to go too. We filed out saying that we'd see him tomorrow, and he smiled between labored breaths. His last gesture to me was one of his little doll-baby waves.

My mother called at one in the morning and calmly said, "Lee, he's gone." We all returned to the hospital and cried and touched his body under the sad light. I kissed his forehead, taking note of that familiar birthmark, and said good-bye. Of course I had known it was coming, but I couldn't believe it. He was sixty-eight.

Brian took my mother home in the wee hours of that morning, somewhere around five, about the time Daddy would have been getting up. In his grief, Brian went upstairs and walked down that narrow gold hallway to my father's workroom, which was now a kind of shrine. There was his Radio Shack monitor, lit up as though it were waiting for Ed to punch in the new day's input. Brian remembered the piece of paper in his pocket, sat in my father's swivel chair, and used the commands Daddy scrawled out for that troublesome kink. He pushed "enter" and the snag unraveled, of course. Daddy had come to the rescue for the last time.

Indeed Ed Pearson was an unlikely hero. He helped his mother by working when his own father died, at an age when a boy really needs a man in his life. He helped rescue our country from Hitler, winning the Bronze Star for bravery during the Rhineland campaign at barely twenty. And he showed up in my mother's life at a time when she'd given up on finding a decent man. Even though I more often played the role of counselor to him and he couldn't remember things like what grade I was in, he never turned down my requests at any age for help. One of the last things he did while he was well was wire my workroom for the kiln I use in my business. When I see his handwriting on the door of the fuse box I always remember how as early as fourth grade I could perfectly copy his signature with its connected capitals "EDP" and tightly vertical "earson."

In my grief a strange memory surfaced. Once, in a rare moment of normality, Daddy did something so fatherly that I could hardly look him in the face. At the end of my junior year in high school, he showed up in the library for my National Honor Society induction reception with an orchid corsage. At the time I was so embarrassed, especially when he wanted to pin the big purple flower on my sweater, which meant I had to wear it all day at school. This was not our dynamic—this male/female, mushy thoughtfulness motif. That's when I realized that despite his idiosyncrasies, unmatched in the history of paternity, I liked him best when he was acting silly and hardly able—no, unable—to contain himself about his projects to whomever would listen. What is even more enlightening, or frightening, is that I may be becoming more like him than I'd care to admit.

It's been nearly a decade since my father died. He went too early—too early to see his sons' weddings and his precious granddaughter, not to mention his wildest electronic dreams come true. For once he was on the cutting edge of something that everyone else would actually know about. Just a couple more years and he would have made it into the mainstream and maybe found some kind of computer job in his twilight years. But whenever Bill Gates holds one of those press conferences where he's standing in front of a blue curtain with a computer, I think of my father. When the silliness bone I inherited from him gets the best of me, I like to imagine Daddy as the computer mogul's boxer-shorted, chicken-legged guardian angel, directing his every electronic idea with a big heavenly mouse.

THREE

looking for my southern womanhood

She girds herself with strength and makes her arms strong.

Proverbs 31:17

Knowing that arthritis and osteoporosis run in my family, I made a millennium resolution to begin regular weight-bearing exercises at our nearby YMCA. Trying to avoid the huge gym full of buffed bodies, I discovered the "Wellness Center," a small quiet room of equipment where mostly elderly members exercise. I like to call it the Matlock Room. These patrons are white-haired, bent over, and about as jolly a group as you would ever want to know. But the women look particularly out of place to me, a girl who grew up watching white-haired women work, not work out. This went beyond curious and became downright disturbing when later I'd walk into the locker room and find one of them naked.

I never once saw my grandmother, a woman born at the turn of the twentieth century in a small North Carolina railroad town, do anything that could be termed athletic. Just the thought of Mema in pants or—heaven forbid—shorts makes me tremble, yet she had the physical and mental strength of an Olympian. Every day at 6:00 A.M. she hopped down from her high four-poster bed and shimmied one of her "work dresses," a sleeveless bodice attached to a gathered skirt, over her five-foot-five, approximately 170-pound frame. Once she laced up her black, orthopedic-style work shoes, they didn't stop moving until about 7:00 that night, except for one fifteen-minute break during the day, at precisely 10:00 A.M., to rock on the front porch and throw back a 6$^1/_2$-ounce Coke. When I, her little suburban granddaughter, visited in the summer, I quickly tired of keeping up with her and usually found a quiet corner in one of the ten bedrooms of her boarding house to play dolls or color.

Mema moved through the house like one of the freight trains that ran through her backyard ten or so times a day. My mother said Mema used to actually move the furniture, by which I mean seven-foot walnut highboy dressers, huge four-poster beds, and wing chairs designed for Andre the Giant, to clean the floor and vacuum the carpets thoroughly. She lifted every one of what my father joked were one hundred lamps to dust underneath. Every Monday, Mema loaded the linens from all twelve double beds into her '65 Chevy and carted them to a laundromat, which was an improvement from the early days when she washed them in the yard in one of the hand-cranked wringer machines. Then, as though bleaching and starching bedsheets weren't enough, she *ironed* every last pair for all twelve beds.

As grueling as Mema's cleaning schedule was, her cooking ritual was enough to provoke insanity. Between preparing the meals for the boarders and washing every last dinner and dessert fork by hand, her thick legs and chunky black shoes crisscrossed the kitchen for well over six hours every day. Plus, she cooked by means of original sources: ripping up chickens at their joints with her bare hands; making yeast dough every morning for Crisco-soaked rolls that night; and occasionally, when I came to visit, cracking open a coconut with a hammer and a screwdriver, draining its milk, and grating the chunks for my favorite dessert, coconut cake. I never once thought to tell her not to go to all that trouble.

In the evening she sat in "Mema's chair," an oversized green brocade one, and propped up her feet on the matching stool, both of which, along with all of the other pieces of furniture in the house, she reupholstered herself. She would needlepoint or knit bandages for a leper colony until 10:00, when she locked the doors, went to bed, read for thirty minutes, and then turned out the light.

It's important to note that Mema had the body for all this heavy work. Granddaddy used to say she had a rear end on her like a twenty-dollar mule, but he meant it in a good way. I know for a fact that she weighed more than he did, and her hands outsized most men's. She walked with her shoulders and head slightly protruded, digging her heels into the floor, then rolling herself forward with every step. Her upper arms hung like silk draperies from a steel rod.

Back at the Y, in front of the omnipresent mirrors of the Matlock Room, I noticed those same draperies pooling around my upper arms. After working out at least three times a week from January to April, my weight had not really changed and I didn't want to hear the line about muscle weighing more than fat ever again. I thought at least my arms would have a chance at being thin, if for no other reason than how much my elbows shook when I tried to lift those big bars of weights. But there they were, the ghostly images of Mema's arms attached to *my* torso.

All of a sudden it seemed pointless to continue this mad routine of simulated walking, cross-country skiing, and bike riding. (Sometimes when I am on the front bike, furiously pedaling nowhere, I want to turn to the old folks on the bikes behind me and yell, "Come on, gang, there's a fire down at the old barn!") How absurd to strap myself up to these modern torture devices when I still looked pretty much like me—a woman more likely to be described as "sturdy" than "svelte."

Yet, really, at my stage in life, happily married and the mother of three, if all I am thinking about at any given moment of a day is a hank of flesh here or a bulge of skin there, my self-image deserves to be pitied. I should wear those hanks as symbols of my true coconut-splitting heritage. Rather than being absorbed in adolescent shame at my shape, I ought to latch on to my womanhood, real Southern womanhood, if such a thing exists anymore. When I think of all the artificial steps I have trod, the whole time watching the electronic tally of how many calories I burned on my stationary journey, I wonder what good it has done me either physically or in my spirit. What ever happened to doing real work, the kind that has a completed project, a clean house, or an immaculate yard as its payoff?

Like Mema, I've got the body for *that* kind of workout, but I'm wondering if I've got the spirit. She would probably fail any of the current women's magazines' pop quizzes on fitness. But when I look back on her life, I see her as a blur of activity—wallpapering, upholstering, cooking, and surviving without ever complaining that she could really use some stress reduction in her life. Even if I just once manage to bring the two sides of the butterfly machine to my sternum, I wonder if I can dig my heels into life, leading not with thin thighs but with a hard head. I think the answer is, "Not yet. Not as long as I want to be somebody else."

Deep down I don't want to be muscular, and I can't even pronounce osteoporosis, much less worry about it yet. What I really want, and what has been tied to every weight-loss scheme since the onset of puberty, is to feel what it would be like to be beautiful, to hush a room, to have, dare I say it, sexual power. But if that wasn't in the cards for me at eighteen, then it won't be dealt to me now. So while I have exercised my self-image into this "revolution of rising expectations," my rear end continues to sink.

Regardless of how hard I work out, I will never have those little chicken arms that look so good on all the women in their designer gowns at the Academy Awards. I'm ashamed to admit that sometimes when I'm watching *Friends*, I just want to take Courteney Cox's upper arms and snap them in two like a little wishbone while wishing for arms like hers. But I must face the truth that my shot at the perfect figure—or more realistically, a better one—is just about over. The only alternative then to achieving more sex appeal is to redefine it.

In Mema's post-Victorian, pre–Victoria's Secret era, it may have been easier to describe one's attractiveness within broad parameters. Perhaps everything about a woman—her sense of humor, her gait, even the softness of her ample arms—defined her sexuality, if it even needed to be defined. So my wide-set hips, my tendency to walk "like a farmer," as my dear mother once observed, or my high energy level should create a connection to my Southern sexuality. Having the rear end of a $20 mule, adjusted properly for inflation, should be a source of pride. So why am I tempted almost daily to squander that heritage of strength in search of a flaccid, two-dimensional womanhood?

Although it could be interpreted as the most convoluted rationalization for eating fudge ever concocted, I am hopeful that adopting new—or perhaps more time-honored—notions of sex, beauty, and strength will free me to be myself, the most effective beauty treatment of all. Besides, I would do well to remember the comment of Mema's more worldly cousin, who once shot back to someone talking about looks, "The sensation is all the same in the dark anyway."

No, I will never hush a room, unless I trip over the threshold on my way in. However, like my Southern ancestors, I can do other things to create beauty in my life. If I am fortunate, like Mema, then spiritual, mental, and physical strength will follow. But Mema did have a certain peachy glow about her. An undeniably beautiful glow, as I recall.

FOUR

sibling natures

Yes, there are many parts, but one body.

1 Corinthians 12:20 NLT

One of the first home movies my father ever took captures my older brother in his crib, bathed in a honey light, smiling right at the camera. He gleefully rocked back and forth with his chubby hands and knees moving like the syncopated pistons that would later come to fascinate him. Once he graduated to two feet, he opted out of walking altogether and skipped straight to running, making it very difficult to get anything but his back on camera. Built for speed, as my mother often said, Dalton raced everywhere—especially toward any object, toy or otherwise, that had wheels. When he got a little car or truck, he didn't just push it around his room or the backyard making cute "vvrrooom" noises with his lips. He preferred to break them apart, even if the effort required tools like a hammer or a rock.

Dalton hammered through the first few years of school too, but by the end of the fourth grade he had become altogether disinterested and simply could not sit still in class. By the end of elementary school, he had memorized every rubber plant and framed print that decorated the principal's waiting room. My parents were utterly baffled by his plummeting grades and increasingly obstinate behavior, and thus began an epic saga of school conferences, punishment, and loud arguments.

While my brother was using rocks to smash dump trucks, I was creating life with them. In the first grade I became obsessed with a big hill on the next street over from my house and raced there as soon as the bus dropped me off from school. This empty lot of pebbles transfigured into my personal quarry of Eden. Each day for about a week, I carefully chose stones of various shapes and hues of brown, loaded dozens of them into my pockets and shirttail, and ran home, slew-footed and hunchbacked, weighted down with body parts. Once back in my tiny bedroom, I glued them into rock people and drew funny faces on them. I'd place each finished man, woman, and child in my windowsill and gaze at them with a serene sense of accomplishment. From then on, I had an insatiable desire to make things. It brought me unrivaled joy to manipulate and control everything from rocks to crayons to my little brother.

Elementary school was created just for me, and I was good at it. I loved to watch my pencil form letters on the page and could sit and write my flowing cursive name over and over again . . . Lee, Lee, Lee. My heart still warms with pride over the papier-mâché Owl from Winnie-the-Pooh I made in the second grade using a small plastic bleach bottle with huge square tortoise shell buttons for his eyes. A poem about Easter I wrote in the third grade garnered a call from my teacher to my mother, and in the fifth grade a small group of us wrote the class play. However, at the time I would have much rather starred in it. That year I had Mrs. Rose, a teacher appropriately named for her honey colored updo, fair skin, and smell of perfume. Since she happened to attend my church, Mrs. Rose and her husband took me out to lunch afterwards a few times that year, which was a heavenly experience for a suck-up. Of course I excitedly told some of my friends on the Monday after this celebrity luncheon, but when the word got out, two girls on the road to roughness took every opportunity to mock me with "teacher's pet, teacher's pet." But as anyone who has ever been a teacher's pet knows, those girls were simply jealous.

About then, Dalton's locomotion hit full stride and he, my father, and my mother had fallen into a Bermuda Triangle of interdependent rage. By age twelve, Dalton and school were not getting along, and by thirteen his taxpayer-financed education was pretty much over—especially since he had discovered his real reason for living.

The minibike, which could be described as a motorized bicycle or a Dalton-sized motorcycle, was new on the market in the late sixties and must have seemed to drop from heaven into our yard as a direct answer to my brother's adolescent prayers. Dalton didn't ride a minibike just for fun any more than a wine connoisseur drinks just because he likes to. He became a collector of a wide assortment of the latest models and a few fine vintage ones, all of which were strewn across the yard, some for riding and some to tear down for parts.

The unasked question for a while was: From where had these minibikes, soon followed by full-grown motorcycles, come? They certainly weren't free, and seventh graders aren't generally known for their ability to pull down the big bucks. Yet more specimens were regularly added to the two-wheeled menagerie piling up behind our house. Before long county patrol cars began making regular visits to our house and a policemen filled in the blanks. I got used to seeing their shiny, patent leather shoes when I peeked through the slats of the louvered screen door before answering the doorbell. Once the officer came inside, my younger brother and I listened out of sight in the hall. After he left, we retreated to my room until the house grew quiet.

Due to his reputation in certain circles of the seventh grade, my brother became something of a cult figure. One of his many wanna-bes was a tall, lanky guy named Hiawatha Ace Jones, who looked for all the world like Linc Hayes on *The Mod Squad*. They and other cohorts did things my inborn fears of getting caught or hurt would never allow me to do. They played chicken one night on two hot-wired bulldozers used during the day to clear a field for a car dealership. They shot BB guns at squirrels while riding through the woods on mini-bikes. Another time they were riding double on a motor-cycle in the woods near a major thoroughfare where a police helicopter just happened to be hovering over rush hour traffic. As Dalton, Hiawatha, and the motorcycle came flying through the trees toward the road, a bull-horned voice from the sky, sounding like God beating his chest, warned them, "Don't go on the street with that thing, boys." That may have been the only time Dalton got a little scared—until he realized it was only the cops, at which point he continued into the intersection and then turned into Hiawatha's driveway. Mr. Jones had been sitting on his porch watching and calmly observed from his rocking chair, "Well, they're coming at you from the sky now, Dalton."

One Saturday during those disquieted years, as my mother stood at the kitchen sink, she looked out of the window to see her thirteen-year-old enraptured in a rare peace. Beginning from behind the corner of the house to her right she noticed a line of metal shapes laid out on the dirt and Dalton pushing an old minibike at the end of the line. He was carefully laying out the last few parts of its engine across the shaded yard. She kept watching as he then retraced his steps, methodically reassembling the small motor for no apparent purpose but his own education. A light bulb or two must have clicked on in my mother's head. A year later the transmission of my father's Pontiac died and Dalton begged Daddy to let him try to fix it. My father gulped when he saw the gears of his car strung out across the backyard but was pretty impressed when his fourteen-year-old put it all back in the car and it worked perfectly.

In anybody's book, this mechanical aptitude was highly unusual for a kid Dalton's age, but when he began the eighth grade no place existed for him in the education system and no one was willing to make one. That was the hardest part for my mother especially—no one understood her son, and no one seemed to care. Consequently, the study of English, history, science, and math had ceased to have any meaning or purpose. As his teachers ran out of patience for his constant disruption, my brother too lost patience and his frustrations finally erupted. Like Tommy Smith raising his fist at the 1968 Olympics, Dalton used his best motorcycle to make a statement, one he hoped would be heard school-wide and particularly by "the jerk," one of Dalton's kinder names for the assistant principal who felt likewise and probably had Dalton's picture on a dartboard in his office.

After school one day, my brother hopped on his vintage Harley, rode up to the high school, and gunned it up and down the wide sidewalks, prompting all the principals to come running out of the office. That ride was listed in the county school administrator's handbook under "Last Straws." The assistant principal told my mother that he would not allow my brother back in a public school—ever. This used car salesman–like educator snidely added to her at the end of the conversation, "Mrs. Pearson, your son makes a mockery of education." After years of butting heads with insensitive guidance counselors and clueless administrators, my mother shot back, "No sir, your education system makes a mockery of my son."

By the end of my elementary school years, I had become something of a counselor to my mother as she struggled to cope. One night as she and I drove into the driveway and the headlights shone onto the family room window, she opened up to me about the family's situation. I don't remember most of the conversation, but her emotions were raw and her nerves were shot over some incident in their Bermuda Triangle. But I'll never forget what she said through her tears before we got out of the car. She quoted my great aunt, saying, "Elizabeth may be right. I don't have a home, I have a battlefield." It was almost a relief to hear her say that, since I had been feeling it. Something inside of me also felt a responsibility to ameliorate her pain and explain everyone's actions, and I even ventured to give her advice. That may have been the beginning of many such long discussions in the future about family dynamics and human nature. I was around eleven or twelve.

When Dalton got his own room, an addition at the other end of the house, I moved from the tiny bedroom to the medium one. This ten-by-twelve space was comparatively enormous, large enough to hold a double bed, a big round table, and four old iron soda fountain chairs. Perhaps out of a need for therapy, my mother became very good at decorating and did my room with a red sculpted carpet, black-and-white check fabric hung creatively on the wall behind my old iron bed, and a fringed white cloth draped over the round table. Every girl's room is her original nest, but mine became a haven. A lot happened at that round table through the years: I created scenes cut out in felt that I glued on black-and-white ticking and framed, pictures made of colorful seeds, and enough Magic Marker drawings to fill the Louvre. I played school with my younger brother or my stuffed animals. With my stereo blaring Elton John or James Taylor, I did all my homework at that table and later wrote my first term paper on an old Smith-Corona. There was a phone jack by my bed, and I spent many hours lying there talking the evenings away with my girlfriends. During junior high and early high school, I was hesitant to have any of them to my house and rarely did. Things were just a bit too unpredictable. Nothing, nothing at all about being alone in my room bothered me. I usually kept the door closed but maintained an open door policy for my mother, who often came in at night to lie down and talk.

The September following Dalton's wild ride, I entered the same school from which he had been banished. Teachers checked the roll twice upon reading my last name and with a shudder would ask, "Wait . . . Pearson . . . Do you have an older brother?" I would meow only a tiny "yes" as she stared at me and made a little pencil marking in her grade book. I offered no details to the connection because this was high school, and by then I craved normality, conformity, popularity, and every other -ity that had to do with fitting into a group. But my shelter, the cleft of the rock, from the turmoil churning in our house would be found in academic achievement at school. Looking back now, I see that I gradually learned to value thinking over feeling because the emotions around me were so out of control. In the debate over whether human beings are thinking beings

51

who feel or feeling beings who think, my money was on the first. I had been growing up in an intensely emotional environment, one that had its own kind of fierce love but also appeared to have insoluble problems during those few hot years. So school was a place of order and control, plus my analytical approach to family dynamics—whether hereditary or brought on by the environment—came in handy in academics, especially in English and history. Since that night in the driveway with my mom, I had grown accustomed to closely scrutinizing behavior, explaining it, and devising potential strategies and solutions. Only once do I recall letting out my own anger in my room. The rest of my early teen years I kept a tight reign on what I considered to be the irrational aspects of being human—emotions—since they seemed to serve no purpose but to upset.

Laughter was not irrational, though. It was salve. With every giggle exchanged behind the teacher's back, every stifled hee-haw backstage during a musical production, and each Password clue from the stellar wit of my yeoman partner Louis Gary during games every day after lunch, I felt just a little more alive. To this day I am thankful that I was a member of a class full of people who valued silliness and worked hard at it. While some classes held car washes and bake sales to raise money, the Class of '76 charged a buck a person and sold popcorn at our own showings of Marx Brothers movies. We made a killing, and Groucho became a symbol of our class.

In ninth grade a history teacher made an offhand comment about how when we walk into old family houses it can be like stepping back in time. He was a Faulkner fan with his own deep Southern roots and the first teacher to relate a school subject to something in my real life. I had felt that sense of "otherness" many times as a child when entering the narrow, black-and-white wallpapered hall of my grandmother's house in North Carolina. When he made that observation, my burgeoning obsession with the past found a form and a like mind. From then on my personal link to Southern history, Mema, would drive my curiosity to learn more about her and that culture with all its social strengths and moral failings. Later, my idealism knew no bounds, and in light of the issues of the late sixties and early seventies, I asked many questions in that same history class that began with something like, "If everyone could just give some of their money . . ." or "Why do countries need borders?" or "Why would a president lie?"

While my intellect came alive innocently enough, the original seeds of genuine curiosity and a search for connection eventually produced a sort of hybrid intelligence plant. Over the years I may have added more than enough fertilizer to my brain out of fear that it would look scrawny and average. This came in part from another teacher I respected who had the habit of referring to former students with labels that implied degrees of intelligence, as in "She is incredibly smart," "He is so smart, it's scary," or "That guy is brilliant, just brilliant." While intrinsically harmless, these labels triggered a competitive bone in my nonathletic body, plus it didn't help that my old teacher, Mrs. Rose, lived on in my heart, encouraging me to find favor with her successors.

Still, while I was striving to be "wickedly smart," I wasn't quite sure at sixteen what that meant. In adolescent hyper-insecurity and once in a while now in adult hyper-insecurity, the criteria for being intelligent seemed to be just about everything that I had missed in my background. The standards I imagined for being "outrageously smart," here presented in note-taking form, were (a) discussing ideas that only existed in a vacuum, (b) academic name-dropping, (c) rapier wits fed by current events, (d) just the tiniest bit of social condescension, and (e) the entire notion of nonutilitarian reading. To this day just the mention of *Little House on the Prairie* books can shake my self-esteem to the core, since it seems I was the only little girl in America who didn't read them.

Although TV factored in to my limited childhood reading (how sad that I'd stop jumping rope to run in and watch *Gidget*), I spent much of my early childhood years in a little woods behind our house. It held the world headquarters of my mud pie production in its "kitchen area." Far down the path was my own secret plot of moss that formed a square carpet between four trees. That was my living room. I remember many days gathering scrap wood for walls and pine needles for beds and chairs, looking up at the sun streaming through the treetops onto the moss, speckling my green carpet with light. This was dirt-under-fingernails fun to me, times of rapture that took away all appetite. Back in the house at night, it would have been difficult to get encouragement to read from my mother since she was fidgety too. About the time we came along, she found herself in the neighborhood garden club, and then really found her inner self teaching craft classes at the YWCA.

For different reasons than Dalton, I didn't make much of an association between my fun in the woods and my education. Although my class schedule always included art, a distorted hierarchy ruled my mind when it came to knowing things versus knowing how to do things. Perhaps I took "doing" for granted since it was all around me at home. As college approached, the goal was to know things—actually, to "know everything," particularly about history and English. And knowledge, the kind college applications wanted to see, had to be backed up with cold hard numbers. Since it's not so easy to measure rock babies and mud pies, the kind of learning that could be quantified by an authorized dealer took higher priority. It is much easier to use intelligence as an ego prop when you have a convenient scorecard that formulates grade point average, class rank, and SAT scores into a handy obnoxiousness quotient.

While I added up my grades and worked the averages in the margins of my notebooks, Dalton worked a forty-hour week as an apprentice at an auto repair shop. But another series of incidents after work led to an opportunity, of the last chance/ultimatum variety, to attend a small program in Maryland that we called "motorcycle school." In a highly unusual show of unity, the entire family dropped him off there, not unlike the first kid going to college. We found the school, saw the boarding house where he'd live, then headed out to the main drag to eat an early dinner at a steak house. No one really talked.

When we'd finished eating, my brother stood up and said, "I'm gonna go now." My father offered to lead him back to the boarding house, a complicated trip involving the Washington Beltway, a challenge even to seasoned drivers. At barely seventeen, having been pretty far in his life already, Dalton made his wishes clear, looking right at Daddy, "I don't want you to. I can find my way back by myself." All the scenes of anger—pounding bathroom doors, red faces, threats of leaving—were forgotten then. This was as much a moment of relief as it was independence. Some kids say good-bye to childhood as their parents walk out of their first dorm room. After my mother grabbed him for a pretty unresponsive hug, Dalton said good-bye to us and just walked out of that cafeteria. As he drove his Camaro past the window where we sat inside, my father's eyes followed him out of the driveway. For the very first time in my life, I saw tears falling down Daddy's cheeks, catching the sunlight coming through the sheer curtains of the restaurant.

Dalton would do fine. The first day of class, he was told to sweep up until the instructor returned. That done, he came upon three or four piles of scrap motorcycle parts in the garage area of this very small operation. As the family folk tale goes, when the instructor returned, there stood two working motorcycles with their creator sitting on one smiling, just like in those old home movies. (That was indeed a folk tale. What Dalton actually did was slip a few of those old parts that he needed for his "out-of-class projects" through a hole in the side of the garage for later use. Some habits die hard.) Needless to say, he finished the motorcycle course in record time and, as Daddy used to joke, *magna vroom loudy*.

I was the first one from either side of my family to go to college, and it was a dream come true for me. My interest in the South went with me, but so did a timidity that too often asked of my school, "Who do you want me to be?" It would have been better to take the consumer approach, using college to learn about my interests and bolster my skills, but that's a fairly unlikely approach for an eighteen-year-old at a liberal arts college. Instead, I pictured the three-story library as a vast ocean of knowledge that I had to drink up, one history book and British novel at a time, according to someone else's syllabus. Only when I swallowed them all would I be full of knowledge, full of myself, and fully worthy of an opinion, despite the fact that the first person pronoun was strictly forbidden.

It didn't happen often, but once in a while, in the midst of so much required knowledge, a piece of literature or an episode in history would resonate strangely within me, illuminating something in my experience or current events. As nerdy as it sounds—and actually is— I enjoyed having a drawer of the card catalog imprint on my stomach as I thumbed through it front to back looking for a book title that spoke to one of those illuminations. I'd run up the stairs with the call letters in my grubby little fist to track the book down in the maze of shelves and would often get a small adrenaline rush when its index contained what I needed. Those small epiphanies made me feel less anxious and more connected to being human despite the inordinate amount of time I spent alone in the reading room of the library. Overall, though, I too often approached my formal education as I had my life—as a spectator. I had mastered the art of secondhand living growing up, and it was a difficult habit to break. I found it much easier to study another's passion on paper than to use my own voice in the real world.

The real world would not wait forever. On a Sunday afternoon in May, the very New England, bow-tied college president pronounced us graduates. He then had to ruin everything by saying, "Welcome to the community of the educated." First I looked backward over my shoulder and wondered if he was referring to me. I had indeed been educated, if taking forty or so courses ranging from anthropology to economics (both of which I still know nothing about) qualified me for a gate pass into that elite-sounding world. My second thought was how that comment sat with my mother, whose other kid got turned away at the entrance of the community of the educated by a security guard.

While college had been a privilege and the right path for me, it would take me a long time to rediscover the kind of intensity that Dalton had for his work. After one more stint of working for somebody else, he opened his own shop, Dalton's Automotive, when he was about twenty-two, the age when most kids finish college. He does any kind of auto repair, especially rebuilding blown engines, but his real expertise is in building racing engines using very expensive, specialized machinery. He does this for his own drag car too, the same '71 Camaro that he drove to motorcycle school and still races, officially or otherwise, all over the East Coast on weekends like he's done since puberty. Dalton has earned trophies for his drag wins and proudly displays his National Hot Rod Association stickers on the rear windshield of his truck. Other drivers come to him for advice, his doctor and lawyer clients hang around his shop gawking and stuttering at his perfectly restored, cherry red '75 Corvette, and a few years ago he apprenticed a young kid as a favor to the worried father. He had to end it, though, when he caught the kid stealing from him.

After I married Fritz and became loaded down with offspring, the long-dormant art gene became dominant again and determined my at-home "career" for the next decade. Slapping clay and mud around my basement workroom felt all too familiar, a sort of primeval connection to some other me, the wide-eyed six-year-old running home with rocks in her pants. Still, as I entered the arts and crafts world as a job, sometimes I would hear a snide Yiddish voice ring in my head, "For this you went to college?" I fought the compulsion to quote Edmund Burke or William Faulkner when giving someone their teapot and two bucks change at an art show, deciding it wouldn't be good for business. In my still twisted notions of brain function, there seemed to be no room for more than one interest or identity. I even felt ashamed at times that I was working with my hands instead of my head, and lamented that because of the demands of real life, I have not been good at keeping up with all things intellectual.

To make up for this perceived shortfall in actual intelligence, I have struggled not to fall into habits of using "artificial intelligence." For instance, using certain phrases, like "basically," as many times as possible in one sentence can be a smartness smoke screen. Basically, if you can throw it in the conversation somewhere, then start your next sentence with "Now, having said that," you can appear to both be thoughtful and possess the greatest of all intellectual qualities, basically the ability to hold two opposing ideas in your head at once and not make a case for either. I also fight the compulsion—like laughing at bad news or saying I know someone I really don't—to say "yes" when a book title, especially current fiction, comes up in conversation and someone looks right at me and asks if I've read it. This is particularly embarrassing when my sons ask me, the former high school English teacher, if I've read one of the classics they've been assigned. I pause, then usually say, "Oh yeah, but it was a very long time ago"—true in only about half the cases. I did recently listen to *Wuthering Heights* on tape while I worked in my studio. Now I see what all the fuss is about!

Education indeed has sibling natures. There is the formal kind for which you get credit, the kind that shaped and fed my personality. Then there is the informal kind, not as easy for me as for my brother. Dalton was lucky in a way, because despite his early square peg in a round hole condition, he knew exactly what he wanted to do and used his then unheard-of hyperactivity to get there. His early authority issues did get him in some trouble with society, but in a strange way his rebellion also may have saved his frontal lobes from the same fate as Jack Nicholson's in the Cuckoo's Nest known as high school.

Dalton escaped with his very high IQ intact and shamelessly pursued his passion. But he was no different from anyone else—however he or she has been educated—who lives in a constructed world of highly personalized knowledge, whether that world consists of ideas, tunes, recipes, laws, diseases, or designs. Even though outside forces, like income and class distinctions, try to inflate or deflate the value of some talents, they are valuable all the same. Other forces, like the fear of failure or closely guarded reputations, can intimidate us from trying something new. Just think: If Thomas Jefferson had been afraid to dabble, we might never have had either the Bill of Rights or the dumbwaiter.

My formal knowledge and my awareness certainly broadened as a result of my college years. A few classes and term papers in which I used my own interpretations are the ones that stand out in my memory and, truth be told, the few on which I got an "A." But I hardly ever think about those years in a strictly academic way, and if I do, it ends up as a brain-racking exercise in trivia retrieval. Usually I am waiting at a stoplight, and I'll drift into, *How'd that French guy's name go—"Monty Skew" or is it "Mont Ask You"? . . . Let's see, to spell the other name for the Middle Ages think medical, "m-e-d-i," then "e-v-a-l" . . . What's the difference between the Hundred Years War and the Thirty Years War? About seventy years,"* and usually end laughing to myself recalling a rare joke I heard from a professor in my major, "Remember, there's no future in history." Then the light will change and I'll move on to headier thoughts, like what to have for dinner. But truth be told, once in a while my glorious nerdiness returns, and I start to pursue an idea for no other reason than ninth-grade curiosity. Even though I have not thumbed through many card catalogs lately, when an idea fascinates me I can feel my brain traveling down those old familiar neuro-ruts along their well-worn paths to discovery.

That will always be the beginning of one's true education—fascination. An idea or problem pops up, usually having some relation to our experiences or our individuality, and we follow it up by a search for answers. The answers or insights usually appear to us out of nowhere, creating the same feeling in our minds that a

mother-to-be feels when the baby in the womb reposi-
tions herself—surprise at the evidence of life within. I
have to believe that this mental jazz is the same regardless of the subject matter. Whether it is building an
engine or editing a story, there's a rush when the chaos
comes to order, when the puzzle is solved. Getting just
the right word, mixing the perfect color, replacing a ther-
mostat, changing inflections—fixing whatever doesn't
seem right—builds a sense of mastery over the elements.
By making connections between the parts of whatever
lies in front of you, the original fuzzy idea begins to take
shape, and with each connection the imagined becomes
a reality. The painting is finished, the story hangs together, the race car breaks a record.

As a little girl, manipulating the elements bestowed
life on me, and when I fell back into art a few years ago
as a way to make a living at home, I found that life again.
Now the piecing together of my life through words is
bringing the same satisfaction. Nothing matches the
sense of release that comes from the creative juices flowing out of my brain, down my arms, and out through
my fingertips. But when some outside force, some "voice
of authority"—a real one in Dalton's case and one fab-
ricated in my mind—enters the brain and those juices
get dammed up at the elbow, the frustration can turn
the hand into a fist. Then it is of no use to anyone.

I see very little of Dalton even though he lives nearby.
On the outside our lives seem to have taken very different paths. But when I get deep into a project or a story
and start biting my tongue like he does, we don't look
so different after all.

grace
IN LOVE

the summer of a lifetime

Love bears all things, believes all things, hopes all things,
endures all things. Love never fails.

1 Corinthians 13:7–8

After just ten days of marriage, Fritz and I landed on
Martha's Vineyard, the tony island off the coast of Massachusetts, on a drizzly June night in 1980. We came
not to honeymoon but to provide morning entertain-
ment for approximately seventy-five children in an
upscale summer community known as West Chop. I did
arts and crafts with the little kids and Fritz organized
games for the older ones while the parents played tennis on the eight perfectly manicured clay courts.

When I woke from a long nap on the ferry ride over,
my eyes were blurry and rain dotted the windshield. As

we traveled from the boat dock at Vineyard Haven out to West Chop, the road dipped down, then up so I could finally focus on my new neighborhood. What I saw looked like a movie set to me, a thoroughly middle class girl who grew up thinking the high life was going to a motel in Virginia Beach each summer. This was an otherworldly way to enjoy the ocean. Three-story homes set on rocky cliffs overlooking Vineyard Sound cut impressive silhouettes in the pinkish midnight sky, and outlines of huge boulders formed jetties out into the sea from the point of land we crossed.

Little Pier, Big Pier, and Middle Pier would soon replace 7-Elevens and shopping centers as my reference points, but on that rainy night, everything was new about this place and about us. We were so young—only twenty-two—and looked at each other with giddy, wide-eyed amazement, an attitude that came easily then. Rounding the corner at a flagpole and passing a stand of small, crippled trees and a rustic inn, we beheld our first home as a married couple—two rooms above the community's tiny post office. Not many newlyweds can say that their first sugar shack had its own zip code.

We were only required to work from nine until noon each day, which for me meant making yarn babies and egg carton caterpillars with the five-year-olds. Fritz had the harder job of keeping mostly nine- to twelve-year-old boys on the run. Once I took my charges on a rock hunt where we looked for the ones I'd painted blue and planted on the beach the previous afternoon and saw Fritz running shirtless across the jetty, sweating, with an intense look of concentration on his face. In a minute or two, six or eight boys came right behind him in hot pursuit. He was in his own kind of heaven.

After those fifteen hours a week and an occasional pet beauty contest, night softball game, or church service, we were done. For that we got to eat gourmet food in the dining room of the inn, free lodging, and two thousand dollars. The whole setup felt less like a job and more like we'd won the big prize on *The Newlywed Game*. In my wildest dreams growing up, I couldn't have imagined such a place. I sometimes wondered later if I wouldn't have been better off not knowing it existed at all.

But now that we were living in this paradise, even though it was as the help, with so much free time, we explored the triangular island before coming back to our post office bungalow to laugh about the precocious kids and their parents. After graduation and the pressure of a wedding, I felt deeply relaxed that summer. In my newfound dissipation, it didn't take long for the island to have its way with me. I loved sitting on the end of Middle Pier in the late afternoons to do nothing but gaze at the aquamarine sky, the blue-black sound dotted with bright white sailboats, and the gleaming black-and-white ferries. From the left the big boats emerged out of a slit in the shoreline known as Wood's Hole and headed around a bend to Vineyard Haven, then back again. The ferries crisscrossed the sound all day like clockwork, but each time two of them came from opposite directions, from where I sat they looked as though they would collide. But they always passed by each other unscathed.

The following summer we decided pretty quickly to take the job again. My college roommate, Liane, came to visit us as she had the first summer, but this time she brought her new boyfriend, Brian. We picked them up in Vineyard Haven from the last arriving boat of the day. After those years spent in our dorm at night talking about guys, I was anxious to meet this man whom she thought was "it." When Brian emerged from the shadows of the old ticket office, I took a firm look at him and knew I'd need a bridesmaid's dress pretty soon.

In coming years, Liane and I would use the island as our touchstone, a place for two college girls who reluctantly turned into women to recapture our roommate closeness.

The entire family had fallen in love with the island, and for the next four summers my in-laws rented a place there, each house becoming a reference point for some milestone. We brought our first son to join the family at the Mill Keeper's cottage on Seven Gates' Farm. The beach across the street from the big white "steeple" house on the road to Vineyard Haven was where our two boys first felt the sand beneath their chubby feet. I met my future sisters-in-law at that house. Its wraparound porch became the site of raucous nights of "Fictionary," a game in which a crazy dictionary word that no one knows is chosen. Everyone then submits an ersatz definition, trying to fool others into guessing it to be the real one. Poppop Fox often won the round, but it was Nana who won for most original. For "mittimus," she submitted amongst our overwrought entries, "Three little kittimus, have lost their *mittimus*." The next day a few members of the very staid, New England seashore village commented in a nice and almost jealous way on the noise coming from the front porch.

After those four summers, getting back to Martha's Vineyard became impossible for one reason or another. It would be ten years before we would return, but when we did, it was in style. Our home for two weeks would be one of the graceful mansions set on the cliff that I first noticed while driving in fourteen years earlier. Its twelve bedrooms full of antiques and hooked rugs, huge kitchen, and open living room easily housed all twenty-seven of us. The view from the backyard was a living painting of the sea with those same sailboats and ferries and the lights of Cape Cod dotting the opposite shore. As many photographs and videos as I took those two weeks, they could never capture the dapple of breeze through my hair or the feeling of rest the heavy salt air brought.

It had been a very long decade, but everything about this place was still recognizable. The problem was I just didn't recognize myself. Those honeymoon days, once so clear, had spun out into the hazy past, replaced by days full of the never-ending demands of three little kids, job and financial stress, and desperate search and rescue operations for my identity. Coming back to the spot of such carefree, uncomplicated days made the weight of responsibility feel even heavier. Also I knew that after the summer of '94 ended, changes would be upon me because of changes in Fritz's status quo. In other words, we were about to take a risk that would send my carefully ordered, predictable world spinning out of my control into a vast unknown. The only thing I felt secure about was that the future promised insecurity. I was ashamed of myself for being so anxious in the midst of such natural beauty. I clung to each hour of those two weeks the way my brothers and I had done those summers so long ago, not wanting time to move any further forward and bring this rest to an end.

Just when I needed her most, Liane came to visit me on the island, just like those earlier summers. She had been on her own kind of odyssey through the decade, living in Texas, Illinois, Washington, Alaska, and by then had just settled in Maine. That summer we met again on Martha's Vineyard and talked for hours at a local tavern about where life had taken us and where on earth we might be going. It was a conversation that steeled me a little but made me realize how much I missed this friend and the kind of intimacy girls share. Liane came into my life when the only responsibilities we had were our studies, and seeing her always reminded me of my younger self. She only stayed overnight and left on the morning ferry. I stood on the same dock where we had met so many times and waved a long good-bye to her and Katie, her beautiful, red-headed, seven-year-old daughter.

Two days later, on the lily-lined yard of that graceful mansion, we celebrated the Fourth of July. As the sun dropped and Venus appeared in the western sky, the tiny white lights of the communities on Cape Cod twinkled across Vineyard Sound before the fireworks display began. Balls of green, blue, and pink mushroomed out of the faraway shoreline in silence. But that wasn't exciting enough for the kids. They were beside themselves to light the ones Fritz's uncle Dave brought from South Carolina in a Hefty bag. In a mini rite of passage, Dave told our twelve-year-old Cheston that he could light the first one, which he did, then ran backwards flapping his arms like wings in wild excitement. Everyone gathered around the Coke bottle and watched rocket after screaming rocket launch into the dark sky. Then Dave announced, "Now for the show stopper . . . the *pièce de résistance* . . . the Battle of Lexington!"

The six little boy cousins from ages two to twelve crowded around the fuse, then drew back when it lit. The family semicircle watched this gyrating mass of fire retell the story of the Revolutionary War in all its red, white, and blue glory until the yard glowed with American history. Afterwards, my little nephews ran through the cold, dark grass in fleshy bare feet, kicking a beach ball until their bodies intertwined into a wrestling match. The air was cool and still. It was a perfect night.

When the excitement ended, my sister-in-law ushered the little cousins to bed. I could see them upstairs in the soft yellow lamplight of the gabled window, those two compact boys in their pajamas pressing their noses against the window screen, yelling down to me. They wanted nothing more than to come back to the yard to be with the adults. I could almost see the memories forming inside of them. As I looked in the living room on the floor below, I saw their grandfather reliving his.

The television boomed out the 1812 Overture as my father-in-law conducted his own imaginary Boston Pops, flailing his arms and pointing his invisible baton to key instruments at just the right moment. It was amusing, yet judging from the serious look on Poppy's face, I am not sure that was his intent. He was in there alone. The stockbroker maestro was lost in the moment as his head bobbed to the thunderous music and his spirits soared like a bottle rocket. Standing on the lawn looking up and down on the two generations, I thought about how a boy dreams of being a man, of shooting high in the sky, and how once a man settles down to earth, he changes back into a little boy.

The yard was now quiet. I turned from the house to look out to Cape Cod and could hear the light, steady lapping of the water down below the cliff. In that cool, starry night, a foghorn blew at regular intervals, marking time like a slow pendulum. As hard as I tried not to, I felt sad at not being able to stop the flow of time and freeze this moment. I thought back to my own little girl summers at Virginia Beach, holding on to my father's clammy barrel back and screeching with delight in the breaking waves. Daddy had been gone two years by then, dead from lung cancer. That summer marked the beginning of my father-in-law's own bout with prostate cancer. My boys were rapidly reaching the age of independence, and I saw the coming years, like the decade before, streak across the sky like three tiny shooting stars.

But rather than bask in the unparalleled joy of that evening and the privilege of being in such a place again, I was borrowing trouble from our future and resisting changes I didn't understand. Then the verse about how love never fails that was read at our wedding came to

71

mind. It was an apt phrase to describe how we got together in the first place. Fritz and I really hadn't been a likely match, but that is God's genius when it comes to romance. We got to know each other the summer before his senior year, which he spent in Williamsburg because of my mistake. I was working in the education office when he called from Connecticut to check on his teaching requirements. The real lady was out of town for just that one fateful day, so I read the rules and, because of a misinterpretation of the words "will" and "shall," told him he'd better get down here right away to take physics that summer. It turned out to be completely optional.

On the first day of fall classes, I saw him in the cafeteria line and felt a little wrinkling in my chest when he said something funny in a soft voice and grabbed my arm and we laughed. It was the same feeling I get now when he hugs me from the back as I stand at the stove in our family cafeteria. It's just that over time it gets harder to see each other purely, as your same essential, youthful self—before roles and responsibilities try to beat it out of you. The real truth was that I was just as crazy about him as I stood on the yard that summer night on Martha's Vineyard as I had been the first time we had laid our eyes on the island. I'd always loved his voice, the way he walked, how he lit up a room with his laugh. We were still like two kids who couldn't stay away from each other, and despite our differences—male and female especially—we were drawn to each other.

But never-failing love goes beyond the romantic and emotional to grip the will. As difficult as it was, I knew that I could not control or prevent change. But the wedding verse also said, "Love hopes all things, love believes all things," which has a sense of the future in it. That Independence night I had to face the future, which I did through a secret path in the hedgerow beside the flagpole. On the other side stood the top of a staircase, built into the cliff, that led over the boulders and down to the ocean. I ventured to the first landing and sat down under the moonlight to gaze out at the black water, backlit shoreline, and starry sky.

No matter how I may have tried to orchestrate time and events into some imaginary perfection, now I needed simply to surrender to the plan for my life without reservation or ulterior motives. I was ready. It sometimes had been all too much, anyway—the insensitivity of time to my plans, how it played hide-and-seek with me, making me search the days for meaning and resolution. Time had finally taught me that no amount of lamenting over change of any kind—from childhood to adulthood, from generation to generation, from being a roommate to being a wife—would quiet the issues growing more noisy in my mind. So sitting on those rather flimsy looking steps overhanging danger, I offered a prayer of surrender over and over again, surrendering my anxieties, and begged to be able to trust the one who made me to see me to completion.

Totally oblivious to my fear or expectation of what the future holds, the earth keeps revolving around the sun and rotating around itself. We seem to stay in one place but are also in a kind of constant double motion, perhaps ourselves being orchestrated into some grand design through imperceptible changes each day. I do know that each year the earth brings summer back to the Vineyard, and just knowing such a place exists somehow gives me courage. We had had the summer of a lifetime, but I was ready to go home. I lingered a while longer, watching the ferryboats. There was something comforting in how silently they arrived and departed, crisscrossing the sound to and from this paradise. But now it was time to go upstairs, kiss the boys goodnight in their attic hideaway, and climb into the twin bed with Fritz.

to an athlete sucking wind

> There are three things which are too wonderful for me;
>   Four which I do not understand:
> The way of an eagle in the sky,
>   The way of a serpent on a rock,
>   The way of a ship in the middle of the sea,
>   And the way of a man with a maid.
>
> Proverbs 30:18–19

Even though I wasn't very educated about sports in high school (at basketball games, I'd yell "REEEE-BOUND!" thinking it was a technical term for "MISS IT!"), I had many male athlete friends. I helped them on their English papers, and in return they got me to ask one of my cheerleader friends if she'd go out with them. Then, over twenty years ago, I came to William and Mary, a school where kids brought physics books to football games. There, of all places, I met and fell in love with a jock—a junior boy from Long Island named Fritz. He was an amazing lacrosse player.

Until then, the only lacrosse stick I had seen was an illustration in the chapter about Native Americans in my history book. But after only a couple of Fritz's games, the sport completely overtook me. The graceful movements, the sheer speed of the players, the impossible saves, and a little random physical violence rid me of any sports apathy. Watching Fritz play, even with his thick black-rimmed "pearl diver" athletic glasses (*way* before that look was cool), fertilized our budding romance. Besides his learned skills, the God-given asset of a low-riding "shelf" rear end gave him ballast and balance and gave me an easy way, besides his number 30 jersey, of finding my new beau on the field. You wouldn't see *me* at a lacrosse game with any books. I had other studying to do.

Fritz was not the biggest player, but he was perhaps the grittiest. The coach called him a "sparkplug" or "Mr. Hustle," while his teammates nicknamed him "Freddy," appropriate since his running style resembled Fred Flintstone's, especially when driving his Brontomobile. Fritz's back would be perfectly stiff, bent forwards a bit, with almost no upper body motion. His stocky legs, like that prehistoric Fred, whirled around in a blur of locomotion. Often he would receive a pass from our goalie, then, in the blink of an eye, he'd be downfield in front of the other team's goal. Once there, he either passed to a teammate without looking at him or held his stick up high directly in front of his body, then "quick-sticked" the ball into the top left-hand corner over the goalie's shoulder.

By the '79 season, Fritz's senior year, I was thoroughly enmeshed in lacrosse and was the only fan to travel to Durham, North Carolina, to watch the Tribe play the

Duke Blue Devils, who were ranked fourteenth in the country. William and Mary arrived on that drizzly April day with an impressive 10-and-3 record but were never considered in the same league, or same breath, as Duke. As the game got underway, Duke soon realized they had their hands full as both teams traded only a few goals throughout the four twelve-minute quarters. Our goalie, Andy Motsko, made one impossible save after another. With less than a minute to go, Duke led 6 to 5. I was standing up, screaming nonstop. As the clock ticked down, Mickey McFadden, a superior attackman, slid in the tying goal. I spun around on the aluminum bleachers in my knee socks, banging my clogs (it was the seventies) and cheering hysterically.

The game went into sudden death. To me, a future English teacher, it seemed a great piece of literature was being written on that muddy field. Only a couple of minutes into overtime, Mickey sealed the win, but a home-field ref called it illegal. The Tribe kept its cool. But then, with all the moral authority that attends a great injustice, Mickey received a pass from fellow shaved-headed (for good luck) captain Chris Royston and cranked the dense rubber ball into history. It was magical, an athletic Camelot. Stick-wielding knights—Sir Mick of Slick, Sir "Nipplehead" Royston, Sir Stops-a-Lot Mots, and my prince, Sir Freddy—had slayed the arrogant Blue Devil. We finished the season 11 and 3. Not long after that game, Coach distinguished Fritz with the honors of Most Valuable Player for the season and a spot in the prestigious North-South game.

Fritz and I married six weeks after I graduated. Except for an annual alumni game, he never played lacrosse again. At twenty-four, we started on our family, and in just four and one-half years had three little boys. Our lives became breathless sprints. We stood in front of our personal goals, not always scoring ourselves, but dodging, with stunned looks on our faces, the speeding balls of duties and responsibilities—diapers and bottles, mortgages and broken cars, homework help and bringing home the bacon. We kept our sense of humor most of the time on this bullet train into middle age, but it has not been without its moments of offense and defense and what seemed to be sudden-death tensions.

But it all paid off when our oldest son was fifteen and life came full circle. He found a start-up lacrosse club and began playing. The following year Fritz found out about a summer league that allowed players aged sixteen "and up" to be on the same team. He decided to support our son by digging out his dry-rotting equipment to play. One early June evening, after nineteen years of dormancy and oh, say, twenty pounds of extra life experience, Fritz stood on the sidelines, buckled his helmet, and ran onto the field of battle.

I brought my folding canvas chair and found a great spot to watch. The other team consisted of mostly twenty-year-old college kids who had all played together on a championship team while in high school. Our team was mostly thirty-somethings and Fritz, then forty-one. But age made no difference. When my beloved emerged from the face-off with the ball, I saw something I had not seen in almost twenty years. Taking off downfield were those Flintstone wheels in full operation. Fritz's rear, although balanced a bit more with weight in the front now, carried him like a middle-aged gazelle toward the opposing goal.

But this time, he passed the ball off, and instead of moving into the goal, he came running towards the coach, waving his free hand wildly in the air, trying to get a word out of his mouth. As he neared, I heard him whisper, "Sub . . . sub . . . I need a sub . . . " He meant a substitute, not a hoagie. Crossing the white line, Fritz bent over, burying his nose into his kneecaps, and a giant

77

sucking sound could be heard up and down the side-lines. This pattern of run, suck wind, run continued through the first couple of games.

But after his stamina had built up, Fritz's old form began to shine. It wasn't long before his wheels sustained him and he got his shot back. There it was, that same high shot into the corner of the goal, right past the lit-tle college boy. Later in that game, another young lion scooped up the ball and started to run up the sidelines cradling it with high-headed cockiness. Out of nowhere the father of my three sons, in a perfectly legal move, slammed the kid with his shoulder, knocking them both out of bounds. Four legs flew around in a circle. When Fritz got up, the ball was in *his* stick.

What symbolic payback. Eighteen years of married life, struggling to catch our breath, and yet we still had it. I jumped out of my canvas chair, pumped my fist at him, and screamed like so many years ago at William and Mary, "YEAH FRITZ! YOU DA' MAN!" I probably overreacted a bit. The woman with whom I had exchanged niceties earlier got up and moved down the field. It turned out she was the mother of the college boy.

Fritz ended that summer season with five goals, a pulled hamstring, a sore heel, and a Vincent Van Gogh of bruises on his right shoulder which he proudly dis-played to everyone on vacation that summer. He also ended up with the respect of our sixteen-year-old who ran the same midfield with his dad and who himself scored a goal during the last game. I won't soon forget the red jerseys—number 30 and number 2—standing side by side with their backs to me, leaning on their sticks as the sun dropped behind a grove of trees sur-rounding the lacrosse fields.

When the players departed the field after the last game, I stayed a few steps behind. I remembered this part of the ritual from those warm spring days in Williamsburg so many years ago. The guys would hang their gloves and pads on the stick and throw the equipment over their shoulders. Walking off—repulsively sweaty, cleats flicking dirt—they discussed how the game went. The girls always stayed a few steps back. I remember how anxious I was back then to change my status from girlfriend to wife. But this summer, it felt good to be a girlfriend—a jock's girlfriend—again.

Right before we got into the car, one of my son's coaches came up from behind us and said, "Nice game, Mr. Knapp. You run pretty good for an o—" He stopped himself, but not before his lips had formed that blasted "O" shape. Fritz did indeed still have it, yet given the physical toll the summer took on his body, I wondered if I would ever see his lacrosse idiosyncrasies again. But the memories of them come back occasionally, especially when we go to Williamsburg in the spring and drive past those fields of glory across from the fraternities.

grace
AT HOME

SEVEN

lunch happens

Man does not live by bread alone.

Deuteronomy 8:3

Every Monday, Tuesday, Wednesday, Thursday, and Friday from September to June for twelve years, I awakened to face three empty, flat-bottomed paper bags standing at attention on the kitchen counter. Having three sons close in age, I figure that I have filled close to 7,940 of them. Many mornings, standing in a pool of refrigerator light, I have probed my finger down the side of the bologna package. Nothing says "good morning" like a slimy meat byproduct. Even before downing my first swig of coffee, I have held many an orange plastic square of cheese (or is it orange square of plastic cheese?) six inches away from my nose, scratching at its middle, trying to unwrap it without losing the corners.

Then, like the most veteran Vegas blackjack dealer, I flip down six slices of white bread and hit 'em once with the bologna, then again with the cheese. Wondering what ever happened to my youth, I drop the sacred elements into the bags while little monks chant through my head: "Drink . . . drink . . . drink . . . apple . . . apple . . . apple . . . sandwich . . . sandwich . . . sandwich . . . Little Debbie . . . Little Debbie . . . Little Debbie . . ."

Imagining the little dears at school happily eating, then rising up and calling me blessed right there in the cafeteria, was the only slim consolation to my martyrdom. That is why it came as a shock when my middle son ratted on his younger brother. They were eating an after school bowl of Lucky Charms, 90 percent of their food pyramid, as I stared out the kitchen window, wondering what to cook for dinner. I heard Eric say, "Stephen doesn't ever eat his apple."

"What!?" I replied, wheeling around on one heel. "Stephen, is that true?"

He raised his spoonful of marshmallow stars and his eyebrows in guilt.

"Stephen, don't you know the apple is the most important part? It's like the . . . the . . . the conscience of the lunch. You have to eat the apple."

It was more for my conscience. It was the one fruit or vegetable of the pyramid section I thought they *had* to eat.

What followed was an eye-opening description of the sixth-grade lunch room that rivaled the Chicago Commodities Market—kids dealing in tuna options and Ho-Ho futures, tangerines and Fritos flying from one end of the table to the other, sold to the highest bidder.

Upon hearing this, existential thoughts rolled through my head like an errant grape on a cafeteria floor. I stood there frozen while the images of a Sherwood Anderson story that I read in college replayed vividly in my head.

Every week, out of the goodness of her heart, an old woman fed a pack of wild dogs in the woods on her way to town. One snowy day, on her way home with sacks of grain, she fell down and died in those woods. The ravenous wild dogs circled around her, dragged her frozen body into a clearing, and ate the grain. In my exaggerated recollection of her tale, the dogs didn't stop there, if you know what I mean.

I am that woman. Despite my role as keeper of the pantry, underneath my white terrycloth robe with the jelly-stained cuffs still stands a warm-blooded woman. Sometimes on cold winter mornings, when I am wrestling with bitterness and with the rubber spatula against the last striations of peanut butter, I wonder if anyone would notice if I slathered the Peter Pan all over me instead? Then, in a twist on that morbid old lady story, I think about just lying down on the kitchen floor in the early morning darkness and calling for *my* dog. There's a story with a happy ending for both man and beast.

I have come to refer to my chore as "The Lunches," as though it were a sixth member of the family or a monster locked in the pantry. Every weeknight at about 9:45, since the nearby grocery closes at 10:00, I say to anyone who may care, "I'll be right back. Gotta get something for The Lunches." When Eric first had his learner's permit, he always wanted to come with me. He'd entertain me up and down the aisles, tempting me in a darn good British accent, "How 'bout some Pup Tots, Mummy?", walking like Groucho Marx, or tossing Fruit Roll-Ups into the basket and yelling "the field goal is up . . . it's good!"

One cool October night, right there in the cereal aisle, I had an epiphany about all this eating. The very seed of relationship—conversation—seems to have some primal connection to food. My revelation was confirmed on the drive home, when this same fifteen-year-old offered me the tiniest but most delectable tidbits of his mind in between my screams of "There's a ditch over here, you know!"

As tiring and monotonous as it can be, raising children happens one slice of bologna at a time, and before you know it, all those Little Debbies and mushy apples have turned them into grown men. Now that they are peeling out of here like bananas, I figure I only have about 800 bags left to fill before all three get their meals from college cafeterias, the line at Burger King, or, if they are lucky, another woman's cellophane wrap. Maybe by then I will have studied all those cookbooks I got for my wedding and will be begging them to come home for a nice hot Sunday lunch. Hopefully, they will forget the sarcastic "chicken or hamburger, chicken or hamburger" debates I carried on with myself at 5:30 every evening of their upbringing and accept my invitation.

EIGHT

canus familiaris

God made the beasts of the earth after their kind . . . and God saw that it was good.

Genesis 1:25

I grew up in a cat family, since my mother's slightly high-strung, catlike personality exuded "no dogs allowed." I think never getting a dog may have had a lot to do with protecting the furniture. We did entertain our neighbor's beagle most every night. I would let Rascal in and play with him until he fell asleep in our den. Even though he was an old don't-bother-me hound, it was hard to let him go out the screen door when my friend Maribeth came looking for him every night around 11:00. I envied dog families, but my chance of getting one was so lottery-like that I didn't even bother to buy a ticket. Instead my brothers and I chased the cats around as they avoided us like we were not worthy. It was difficult to even picture myself owning a dog.

Then I got married and met Goody, my in-laws' golden retriever, who came with papers from a well-known breeder in Connecticut. She entered the Knapp family just a few months after me, and I first laid eyes on her at the beach where we were working that summer. I stood back and watched, like I'd done so often around dog families, as this gangly, auburn puppy garnered so much of everyone's attention. My mother-in-law let her off her leash, and we all laughed as she cantered on those huge paws down the rocky shore, then upon hearing Dad whistle turned on a dime to come back. My youngest brother-in-law, Chris, about twelve at the time, played with her nonstop, throwing a ball into the ocean where the beautiful dog would swim to get it. Then Goody would slap the ball down on the sand in front of Chris's feet, collapse her front legs, and look at him with those big brown eyes as if to say, "Do it again, boy. Do it again." You're not going to see a cat do that anytime soon.

Over the years Goody and I watched each other grow into womanhood. While I was producing a litter of three boys under some false assumptions about birth control, Goody gave birth to nine sons and six daughters under contract with a breeder. Both of us experienced some hip displacement afterwards. When our young family invaded Goody's domain, she was always kind. I can picture any one of my children, only a little taller than she, slapping her behind with a chubby hand while casually sucking down apple juice out of his plastic bottle with the other. I'll never forget coming downstairs to find Goody sprawled at the bottom of the steps with three-year-old Stephen in a diaper and T-shirt nestled into her auburn chest, baby and beast fast asleep. As they breathed in tandem, I wondered if they might not be dreaming of balls, a few treats, and how they really disliked being patted on the head.

During those early years of getting to know my in-laws, I noticed what a special relationship my mother-in-law, "Nanny," carried on with Goody. She talked to the dog often, which struck me as a little odd, since I was from a cat family. Even with five sons to feed, she made sure the dog got her food first. I was paying close attention to how my new mother-in-law handled her role as the only female in a house full of men, since I was in the same situation, and it looked like Goody was a big help. So once people potty training ended, it was time to get a dog.

The first place we looked was at a Society for the Prevention of Cruelty to Animals safe house, a private home where puppies stay until they are adopted. The one we were told about was a little farmhouse with acres of property. The owner ushered the five of us down the basement steps as she told about one dog she had in mind. Just as I got downstairs, a rather mangy, full-grown, spotted dog—not puppy—greeted me. This was not the pet I had in mind, and I started rethinking the whole idea and worrying how to get out of it while not appearing heartless in front of this ultimate dog person. Just then a white ball of fur came trotting around from behind the steps. Now this was a puppy. She had cocoa-bean eyes, perky triangular ears, and more than a little attitude. It was love at first sight. Knowing I wanted an antique-sounding name for my new girl, despite the rigorous objections of all the men in the house, I named our new pooch Mabel.

If Goody's manner bespoke country estate, Mabel's shouted trailer park. I know this is our own fault because we missed those crucial early years of training, probably because we were still working on the kids. Consequently, Mabel only comes if I get the loaf of bread off the top of the refrigerator and crinkle up its cellophane wrapper, a trick I use daily to get her to stop that obnoxious barking in the backyard and get in the house. That brings up another terrible habit of Mabel's: begging. This is completely my fault. All she has to do is flash those sad brown eyes at me and I'm toast, so I give her some. It could be some deep psychological compensation package, making up for never having my own dog during childhood, but it is not uncommon for me to throw a piece of people food backwards over my shoulder when no one is around and say, "Oops. Look, Mabel, it's your lucky day."

Mabel's really, really bad habit is eating off the counter. She indulges herself mostly when we are not looking, like in the case of the entire box of Krispy Kremes, although I have caught her plenty of times. How she can lift just the front of her body and crane her neck halfway across the counter to get that peanut butter and jelly sandwich when I turn my back beats me. The way she contorts her body, she almost deserves whatever is driving her nose crazy. And as far as her personal waste disposal, she is pretty good, but she has no modesty issues—the basement rug is just as good as the far back part of the yard. I have heard that some dogs go to the bathroom in the same place every time. For Mabel to do that would be like an elephant being able to ride a skateboard.

The same white fur that made her irresistible as a puppy has since become my hobby. It appears to extrude right from the baseboard molding when my back is turned. Lately I find that I am spending way too much time thinking about the fur and vacuuming it up. Walking around the house I just keep saying to myself, "Look up, look up. Keep your eyes off the floor. You'll live longer." It's easier to ignore the fur on the floor than the strands that hang out over all our clothing, though. We pick white hair off each other like pairs of preening monkeys on the Serengeti Plain.

I have made the mistake of taking Mabel in the car with me a few times. It is irresistibly funny to watch her try to maintain her balance on turns or plant her front legs on the seat at a sudden stop, but her hair gets all over the car. Now that we own a light gray van it's not so bad, but when we had the old burgundy one, the upholstery ended up looking like sheepskin. A few days after one of our car outings, one of the older men who loads groceries in the car for customers at my local store rearranged my thinking on the hair and on life.

This diminutive Italian man with a very calm demeanor placed the bags in the car and said, "I see you have a white-a dog-a."

I responded with a vibrating-lip phrrrumph noise, "Oh yeah, she is quite a mess."

His kind small eyes caught mine, and with Old World lucidity he replied, "Dat's okay. You know . . . da tings in life dat-a bring da most pleasure always make a mess-a."

It wasn't often that a grocery store worker waxed philosophical while packing the Pringles and Cap'n Crunch in the minivan. But he gave me some food for thought. On the drive home, I made a mental list of pleasurable things. Sure enough, I couldn't think of one pleasure that didn't involve cleanup. If messiness indicates pleasure, I have had more than my share. But his comment balanced my growing tendency to be high strung with a renewed appreciation of the pleasure that messy boys and a hairy dog bring. Cats are fine, but they will not challenge you in letting go of the control over your physical environment.

Over time, Mabel and I have grown as close as Goody and Nanny used to be. We have had a good history together and, as they say about old married couples, we have come to resemble each other in some ways. She is truly my *canus familiaris*. During the early child-rearing years, I empathized with her look of longing to escape the quarter-acre plot of land she had been assigned. Those few (daily) times she escaped through the old baby gates and chicken wire barricades we jerry-rigged became her adventures, a secret life we knew nothing about. I knew well the feelings she had once she got her freedom from our suburban yard. Watching her prance down the road smelling blades of grass and lampposts reminded me of those rare Saturday mornings without the encumbrance of kids I spent sniffing out yard sale bargains or playing tennis. I must confess that I have envied the convenience that Mabel enjoys in using all of the outdoors as her public restroom.

I used to make my own barbecue until I asked myself why. It required the slow cooking of a piece of pork known as a Boston butt which produced more fat than meat, making the large, dense bone especially tantalizing to a dog. When I'd dangle this *chateaubriand* in front of Mabel's nose, she adopted a look like she was at confession. Her brown eyes seemed to grow larger as they glanced back and forth between the bone and my face. It was as though my kindness was inexplicable to her, leading her to repent of all the carpet stains, of all the stolen people food, and for every last clump of fur to drop from her coat. After enough of her silent groveling, I would extend the butt of kindness and she'd very gingerly anchor it between her teeth before slowly descending the deck steps and disappearing into the shrubs.

Once clearly ensconced in the boxwoods, she reverted to her dog-eat-dog mentality. We'd see her through the branches, lying down with the bone firmly between her two paws as she licked and gnawed. If one of the boys got within six or eight feet of her, she turned into Bette Davis, snarling and growling with one raised eyebrow.

Watching her become so possessive of the Boston butt bone tickled my funny bone. But it was no laughing matter when later, when I was sure that all the men were asleep, I'd spin the revolving spice rack around to the front of the cabinet. Looking over my shoulder, I'd very quietly unwrap a Hershey bar with almonds and gnaw at it during Letterman's monologue.

As Mabel and I were growing closer over the years, the time that Nanny and Goody shared was drawing to a close. They had been through a lot together. Each year after that first summer when she ran like the wind up and down that beach, the house became quieter and fewer and fewer pairs of tennis shoes were left out in the family room. Nanny and Goody, the two senior Knapp women, regularly stood beside each other on the driveway and watched as each of the four younger brothers hopped into a car and drove away to college and marriage and states from Massachusetts to California. In the blink of an eye, no more boys were around to throw the ball with her, but by then she wasn't all that excited about going to get it.

The years were catching up to the old dog, as I often feel them catching up to me now. As three of Nanny's five sons began families, Goody was very tolerant but preferred to be left alone in a corner somewhere. Near the end of her life her back legs barely supported her weight and cataracts slowly blinded her. To navigate around my in-laws' house, she bumped into furniture, backing up and moving forward as though she were being run by remote control, like a toy car from Radio Shack. At Christmas dinner a few weeks before she died, I looked from my spot at the end of the table into the dark bathroom across the hall. Goody's rear was toward me, and her head was hung over the edge of the bathtub. She was frozen there. Like all of us near the end, she just needed some help getting out of the bathroom.

After Goody passed, I looked at Mabel a bit differently. She is not only a wild animal living in our home, as Fritz often jokes. Nor is she just an endless source of those little white toupees that outline our wooden floors. At times I feel she can only be explained as a gift meant for pleasure and companionship. In my more off-the-wall moments, she stands (or lies around) as a fairly airtight argument for the existence of a pretty interesting God. Really, what good does she, or any dog, do? As unorthodox and downright crazy as it sounds, I sometimes see God's nature and sense of humor more in Mabel than I do in people. Plus there's that whole backwards spelling theory.

Despite the time I've lost—probably years—tending to her food, grooming, health, and bathroom needs, Mabel has taught me by her example how to relax. She single (or quadruple)-handedly rid me of my innate compulsion to control everything. Mabel also has shown me how to stay patient around men. She hasn't minded the boys making her play imaginary drums, dressing her up in clothes, or throwing blankets over her head to test her intelligence, a test which she passed with flying colors, I might add.

As the boys turned into teenagers, Mabel remained the focal point of affection, the target of everyone's need to still baby something. I would not trade anything, even clean floors, for all the times I've stretched out on the family room carpet with one or more of the kids, making goo-goo talk to her as she looks at us like we are her pets. But now that I have stood on the driveway and said good-bye to my two sons as they went off to college, I'm going to need her to baby even more. For as long as I can recall, everyone, including Mabel, has had a place in the family room. But I see the day coming all too soon when she will have her pick of chairs to be shooed from. When her time comes, God forbid, she'll always be a symbol of the messy and exuberant times, our family's age of innocence. But at seventy-seven dog years, her exuberance is waning. More and more all Mabel seems to care about is following the rectangle of sunshine that flows in from the family room window and framing her tired body inside it. The afternoon sun warms her fur while perhaps she dreams of the old wrestling matches, dropped pizza crusts, and high-pitched giggles.

jungle fowl

For you were called to freedom, brethren. . . . But if you bite and devour one another, take care that you are not consumed by one another.

Galatians 5:13, 15

When my oldest son Cheston was in the seventh grade, his science class incubated some chicken eggs. He came in from school one day begging me to let him bring home the contents of a couple of them once they hatched. I softened when he told me the teacher promised this was just a foster situation. We would not be expected to become permanent poultry parents since, as her letter explained, once the chicks reached "a level of maturity" she'd take them out to a farm. I really didn't like the open-ended nature of that definition, but when fluffiness is involved, it is very difficult to say "no." Mrs. Jones, we'll call her, seemed trustworthy, even if she had scared the daylights out of me on Back-to-School Night with her beady eyes and tough-girl swagger. She looked like she had been the kind of girl that in middle school I crossed the sidewalk to avoid.

On the big day, I was to meet Cheston after school and be prepared to transport the bird babies. Walking up the sidewalk, I spied him pacing back and forth in front of his science classroom like an expectant father. He was beside himself with excitement, flapping his own wings like he'd done since he was a baby. Inside the room were a couple of aquariums with lights that warmed about twenty tiny feather balls. In that seventh grade biology class, I saw a perfect example of survival of the fittest when a very big, blonde girl elbowed Cheston and grabbed the last soft yellow, Disney-looking chick. By the time he could get his hand in, only two black, speckled ones remained. Even if they were a little homely, those two were welcomed into our family—temporarily. We put them in the Egg Beaters box I'd gotten from the grocery store to serve as their car seat, crib, and playpen. At stoplights on the way home, I kept looking in the back to see Cheston gazing dreamily at his new pets. The whole chicken homecoming was very tender.

The birds stayed in their box on the ping-pong table downstairs, and a high intensity light we attached on the side brought them to life. They looked so cute when they scurried along the perimeters of their box and pecked at their food, something called "laying mash" that I finally found at an agricultural supply store. When we cuddled the little black tweeties close to our chests, we could feel their fast, tiny heartbeats. I was actually beginning to relax in my new role as poulterer.

That was the fun stage of their development—when they were safely confined in their little box just giving love, not resisting us. But that didn't last very long. They grew quickly and in the blink of an eye passed into puberty, which was the not-so-cute stage, especially when I'd find handfuls of laying mash covering the new basement carpet. As with most adolescents, they would be better off outside. So we converted an old metal puppy cage into a coop. The speckled duo joined the rest of nature outside during the day doing the original funky chicken, happily hopping and flapping all day long in the puppy cage. Every night one of us dragged the cumbersome thing just inside the door that opens to the basement.

This setup worked well until one spring morning when I came downstairs and did not see the cage anywhere. There must have been a failure to communicate somewhere down the lines of family command. With only a sip of coffee yet in my head, I opened the back door and started up the chirpy-talk. "Hey chickie, chickies, gooood moor-ning . . . what 'ya doin' out . . ." But when I leaned down to look in the cage, nothing was there, but the cage door was unlatched. Puzzled, I checked the side of the house, but no chickens. Coming around to the back again, I noticed one lone speckled feather caught in the cage door, ominously twisting in the wind. It seemed we'd been visited by a poultrygeist. Prone to wooziness in medical matters, I didn't want to check the cage or backyard more closely, fearing I might see something resembling the paper-wrapped innards of the Thanksgiving turkey.

The fact was the birds were gone and weren't coming back. I'd probably eaten several thousand dead chickens during my life, but this was different. I knew these two personally, and what is more, they were my responsibility. For a while—maybe two hours—my guilt over not being there for them paralyzed me. I should have been more aware of their whereabouts that night. While I slept away, the innocent little birds were in a fight for their lives, a fight they lost. When I confessed my failure to a few friends, they suggested a raccoon, or maybe a cat, as a likely predator. Someone even mentioned a weasel. My stomach still drops to my knees when I remember that morning. Why was I so lax and not more aware of the danger? It may have been that suburbia, a place where nothing *seems* sinister, lulled me into a false sense of security.

The hard part was breaking the news to the boys. It was a lesson in the cold hard cruelties of life, cruelties that explain why some nature shows issue warnings about kids watching them. As cute as baby creatures can be, they eventually grow up and get hungry for blood, or they themselves get eaten by something bigger or more cunning. Of course we didn't go into such detail with the boys, instead euphemizing the chicks' demise (and my culpability) by saying, "Now boys, the little chickens escaped." After a moment of silence, the boys went on their way. That was one time when having all boys paid off. I'm sure I wouldn't have gotten away with being an accessory to murder so easily if we'd had girls. But the very hardest part came in figuring out how to tell the scary science teacher. I literally chickened out and told Cheston to tell her that our pair "just didn't make it."

It wouldn't be long before the law of the jungle would be adjudicated again, only this time it was inside the house. Cheston had grown into puberty and would soon be leaving middle school for high school. High school! Where had the time gone since I sat in a wheelchair with him in my lap, waiting for Fritz to bring the car up the hospital driveway? What happened to the days since I looked all over town for a special formula for him? And where did that strawberry blonde, blue-eyed, six-year-old Cheston go—the boy who loved to scurry around the backyard, chase his brother with the garden hose, and make a rope swing for G. I. Joe out of willow branches?

He was always such a happy little guy and unusually conscious of other people's feelings.

During middle school Cheston took up skateboarding and loved it, but in that group he stood out about as much as barnyard chickens in a suburban backyard. They were some of the rougher-looking kids in his grade, as well as some much older, who congregated anywhere there were good curbs, steps, or flat surfaces made of concrete. I carted him around to meet up with these guys who had stopped walking a long time ago, preferring to roll everywhere they went. They were a far cry from kids Cheston had gone to elementary school with, ones whose parents I knew well, but that group had its own issues, and besides, they didn't like to skateboard. If I dared bring up any concerns, my cute little darling turned into Alan Dershowitz, accusing me of judging and "just not liking skateboarders." It wasn't that. It was how much more "advanced" they seemed and how naïve he was by contrast. I tried to hide my uneasiness and keep an open mind to these kids, and I grew to like many of them.

But late one August night before ninth grade started, one of them, a Stallone-type with acne, big muscles, and facial hair, called Cheston on the phone. I would find out later that he was cussing and yelling, accusing Cheston of insulting his girlfriend by calling her a name (rhymes with "mutt"), a word my son could not have defined then if his life depended on it, and it clearly did. The boy then told Cheston that he was banned from their group and that he had told everyone what a liar he was and that they shouldn't hang around him anymore. All of this happened as I was in my workroom, alone with my thoughts, completely unaware. But I was so glad to be in place when it was over.

Cheston came down the basement steps to my studio right after the call. He didn't say anything at first, but by his big, unblinking eyes I could tell something was wrong. He looked like he was trying to decide if telling me were cool or not, but before he could say anything, tears began rolling down his face. He sat up on the swivel stool at my workbench and grabbed a piece of soft clay to knead between his fingers. Dying to know what was wrong but not wanting to appear too eager, I kept focused on my painting. After a few seconds of silence between us, it just took a simple "What's the matter?" to open the doors to his heart. Then I saw the little boy I'd been missing for a while, only with a big difference. Now he'd been really hurt. But amidst the pain shone little glimmers of maturity and a completely new dynamic between us.

He told me the bare facts of the case and I quizzed him on some of the background. Then he began to philosophize. "I don't know if I will ever be able to trust anyone again."

Trust? I thought. *He knows what "trust" means?*

"I don't have anyone who I could really call a true friend. Everybody just sits around now and talks mean about other people. We hardly ever even skate anymore. They always make fun of me because I don't like to do that. I want to skate."

We had never talked like this, and I didn't want him to stop. I grabbed a tool and pretended to work and just listened, wondering whether and when to jump in and how long this would last. This was one big dividend after years of payments into motherhood mutual funds. I had to take several deep breaths.

He went on, "If I say to one of those guys, 'Hey, nice ollie' [a trick that makes your board levitate off the ground] or 'Way to land that four-set' [four steps jumped at once], one of those guys will call me a wimp. Anything I say they call me a wimp or just make fun of me. It's no fun. It makes me want to be quiet and never do

101

anything that they can make fun of. It's not like it used to be in sixth grade when everyone could just be themselves. Back then everyone was free."

Wow, I was thinking. *This is so cool. We are actually having a deep conversation.*

Yet again I had to remind myself that I was a mother and that this boy might just be looking to me for a little help. This was all such new territory, but soon our exchanges became more natural. That summer night I told him how miserable my eighth grade year had been because of two girls who did all kinds of things to "leave me out," which was the worst. To be rejected and miss out on a fun time or even a funny comment that everyone will be talking about at school the next day was a felony offense in middle school law. The more I thought about Cindy and Wendy, the angrier I got. How dare they say they weren't going to McDonald's, then I find out they did go, without ME? But that was 1969, and we were talking about Cheston here. We agreed that night that he should avoid returning the sarcasm and criticism, especially since I had seen the size of the other boy, but it might be time to venture out a little and meet new people.

After about an hour of this edibly sweet conversation, he hopped off the swivel stool and let out a big sigh. Still looking for his cues, I smiled at him. With only a little hesitation, my fourteen-year-old came over to give his old mother hen a hug. In the embrace, I could feel his heartbeat against me and marveled at how mature he seemed that night. I also felt sad at how tough it is to let him out to run free in the world.

Cheston went off to bed, but I was still wound up from what only mothers, and especially mothers of teenage boys, would call "excitement." I was thinking about how his predicament mirrored what can happen on into adulthood. Indeed, finding a place to fit in without becoming a predator or a victim of other people in the process is a challenge. I hated to tell him that the pressure to act how others want you to act, to squelch your personality in the presence of more self-conscious ones, only increases. When he said "back then everyone was free," for some reason my mind flashed back to one day at the lunch table during my middle school years. Three friends and I got on a Lorna Doone cookie jag, using the name in culturally pertinent phrases of the times, laughing more hysterically after each one: "You bet your sweet Lorna Doone," "Goodnight Chet, Goodnight Lorna Doone," "Four score and seven Lorna Doones ago," and, shaking our jowls and making peace signs with our fingers, "I am not a Lorna Doone." It doesn't get any better than that. It hit me that night how long it had been since I'd had a really good Lorna Doone moment.

It *is* difficult to stay happy with yourself inside and still be sensitive to others. It is difficult, if not impossible, to stay in the sixth grade and be free and crazy the rest of your life. At some point we all enter the eighth grade. But no one says we have to stay there. Sixth grade—"when we were free"—is a state of mind. If we choose our friends wisely, staying away from weasels and raccoons, then we won't need to chicken-fight our way through life. It also doesn't hurt to turn the other cheek (or gizzard, as the case may be) when relationships change in time or focus and feelings may be hurt along the way.

Maybe my Nature Channel assumptions about that lone speckled chicken feather blowing in the wind can be rethought. Rekindling my own childhood imagination, I should not think of those chicks as helpless victims. I should picture them as mythical heroes, sort of Frank Purdue phoenixes, who on that spring night did not shrink in terror and lose themselves to the law of the jungle but instead pecked the cage door open. Maybe the birds got a running start, spread their wings, and did something no other piece of poultry had ever done before: They flew. They listened to their hearts, screwed up their courage, caught a draft, and soared right over our paranoid neighbor's privacy fence. Those two birds of a feather sticking together would use their wits and develop a sense of grace to escape losing themselves. With all that working for them, they could rise above any real or imagined threat and be free to live out their lives without someone trying to bread their parts and slap them into a deep-fryer with the rest of their kind. That is what I wish for my chick Cheston too—and his old mother hen.

grace
WITH CHILDREN

olives shooting around my table

Your sons will be like olive shoots around your table.

Psalm 128:3 NIV

The funniest thing about being pregnant, besides my general appearance, was how other females felt compelled to relay the grim details of delivering their babies. I'd listen to these women with my arms folded across my basketball belly and feel like I was on a speeding train headed for a canyon where the bridge had collapsed. Just imagining childbirth pain obsessed me as it was, and those self-indulgent horror stories didn't help, especially since they always ended with the pregnant heroine resisting—and badmouthing—an epidural painkiller. I hadn't even had the kid yet and I felt like a failure and a wimp because I knew I was going to take whatever drugs were offered to me at the first twinge of a contraction. To lighten the mood after too many of these female equivalents of war stories, someone usually brought up for comparison the birthing habits of Native American women who in the old days simply "squatted in a field." So now besides knifing pain I also had to worry about the baby just slipping out on a bus or in the grocery store.

But I never got to use any of their helpful hints. As would be the case often in my parenting efforts, things did not go according to plan. After nine months and fifty pounds, with my due date a week away, I had complications. If I were telling a pregnant woman, this is about when the excruciating medical details would start, but suffice it to say a bad case of toxemia necessitated a C-section. I will never forget the doctor saying, "Okay, you'll feel a little tug," which I did, and then, "It's a boy!" That would happen three times in a row, and each time I felt a little tug all right, and still do on a regular basis. But at those three birth moments, my heart was racing, Fritz was crying, and it hit me that all those months it had been Cheston, Eric, and Stephen balumphing around in my stomach, kicking and rolling, not just any old baby. As a friend used to say, "If I'd known it was going to be you, I would have been even more excited."

It wasn't so exciting, though, when a noise like a cat choking rattled in from the second bedroom of our little rental house at 3:00 A.M. Once the irritating bleat fully penetrated my pillow-sunk gray matter, my eyes would open wide with a start, and I'd realize its seven-pound, thirteen-ounce source. Especially the first time around, with Cheston, my long-cherished personal space and self-concept needed a few adjustments. I kept waiting for the primeval maternal instinct to kick in—the one that was supposed to jolt me up out of bed and send me running to the crib singing "Hush Little Baby"—but it never happened.

Mothering, at least the parts that involved physical needs, did not come very naturally to me. That's why for the first few weeks I had to do geometry proofs in my head to convince myself that the irritating noise had anything to do with me. The very first night home from the hospital, a voice sounding like Frankenstein walking through my forehead at 2:00 A.M. told me, "Baby crying. Needs mother. Oh, *I* am mother. Put feet on floor. Walk. Sling breast into baby's mouth."

Perhaps as a result of this sleep deprivation or severe naïveté about baby ownership or both, I briefly wondered about the possibility of raising a faultless child. These ideas weren't fully formed and certainly were not the seed of some grand design for the boy. They were very sub-level, looking for a place to park in the third basement of my consciousness. But when the little ball of flesh was lying there on the changing table, he did seem like what Rousseau called a *tabula rasa*, a blank slate upon which society, or a parent, can write a life. So even if this little baby weren't the result of an immaculate conception, maybe we as his diligent parents could perfectly mold him by closely monitoring his nutrition, utilizing the latest trends in child psychology, and utterly controlling his social and physical environment. A friend used to tell how she warned her three older boys not to tease the baby because they could "ruin" him. Perhaps that's where I got the short-lived notion that if babies could be ruined, then they must be pure to begin with.

Those theories actually found some evidence in the culture of child rearing, which told me I was on to something. Perhaps the evidence was really just marketing—as is everything in America—the first step of which is to create a need you didn't even know you had. Because they see an empty chalkboard across the baby's forehead and feel a tremendous responsibility to write all the right things on it, new parents occupy their own category in advertising circles, one known as "Biggest Suckers." Baby tools like crib mobiles of the periodic chart, pre- and postpartum Mozart tapes, baby food makers, and so on, when combined with a perky mother, seemed to guarantee a smiley and brilliant child.

I witnessed the product of this methodology once, and it scared the daylights out of me. Leaving a friend's apartment in Washington, D.C., when Cheston was not yet two, we met the neighbors on the lawn, a Japanese woman and her baby, who was also around two years old. The woman still spoke in broken English, but her mini-man son had no problem telling us the name of the vice president who served with each U.S. president that his mother called out. In her accent she'd quiz, "James A. Gahfield?" and this chubby little guy would answer in baby tones, "Chesta A. Artha." Then she asked, "Chesta A. Artha?" Showing us his stuff, he grinned back at her, "Nice twy silly mother. Chesta A. Artha have no vice pwesident." Then they shared a giggle. The two-year-old could have been wrong for all I knew, but it was still depressingly impressive. Here she had been grooming her toddler for *Jeopardy!* while I was still struggling with how to get those plastic bottle liners down the tubes and filled with milk without clogging up the nipple so no air would get in the baby's tummy, which *I* would pay for later that night.

As the boys were growing up, the glut in the parenthood advice market only got worse, sending the value to rock bottom. Just like with pregnancy, certain people both locally and nationally felt an irresistible compulsion to relay experiences with their kids—this time *ex utero*—and form universal methodologies from them. It started with a book someone gave me that had a picture of a woman on the cover who could have been a cross between Nurse Ratched and Dick and Jane's mother—tight perm, shirtwaist dress, cat-lady glasses. I should have tossed it in the trash then. She held to the theory of letting the baby just cry himself to sleep, even if it takes hours, so he doesn't get the idea that he can manipulate you. But I couldn't help thinking, *He's a baby, for crying out loud!* I tried it for about twenty minutes before gladly letting him manipulate me so I could get some sleep.

Even though no one would ever admit to believing in the blank slate, I was still picking up signals being broadcast by professionals and amateurs alike—indistinguishable at times—that tried to instruct me to raise my kids in a certain way. Some were helpful, but many of those warnings instilled an inexplicable panic in an already somewhat uncomfortable mother. The advice bullhorn blared out the pitfalls in the high stakes parenting game over the radio, in books, in church groups, and most loudly from other mothers standing next to me on the sidelines of the soccer field. In those early years, I picked up that grooming kids for a life without mistakes and according to schedule relied on a lesson learned in sports too: The best offense is a good defense.

Since I didn't grow up with much childhood programming, this method of preemptive parenting looked like a good idea. Trying to squelch my own seemingly vain personal pursuits, I did my stint as camp counselor mother, the one who sleeps with the minivan keys clenched in her fist. All the sports were genuinely fun, full of adorable moments of personal triumph and cutthroat competition, plus the kids really loved being with their friends and having their dad coach them for innumerable seasons of soccer and YMCA basketball. But when the conversations among the adults turned to serious discussion about levels of players and teams and words like "sacrifice" and "commitment" were used with

111

grade school kids, I got nervous. After one third grade tryout where mean-looking coaches walked around with clipboards grading players, I was convinced that sports were becoming a means to some end. I couldn't help but laugh at how the most ambitious parents talked a little too much about "just having fun." I often wondered what so much organized fun and such close monitoring of every imaginable influence on kids was supposed to ensure. Was it moral purity, or civil obedience, or possibly immortality?

Being prone to take responsibility and control where none is needed anyway, I often found myself in a trance on my way to a soccer game, laboring under some ridiculous guilt and jealousy of other mothers who seemed to have their act together. But by that time, it was way too late. I had bounced off the "ought to" trampoline into the bushes long ago. Out of exhaustion I gave in to my own "style" of motherhood which—like pregnancy—is a whole lot more fun when you don't feel so nauseated.

First I failed the biggest litmus test—breakfast cereal. The voices of authority hummed one major nutritional mantra: Sugar was the devil. We complied with the Cheerios and Wheaties mandates until I was dying to have some Cocoa Krispies again. From then on the boys' tolerance for "white death" was tested up and down the cereal aisle, from the harmless fun of Honey Nut Cheerios to the perverted decadence of Cap'n Crunch. The only time I noticed a chink in their sugar armor came at the spoon of a short-lived brand of brightly colored dinosaurs, maybe in the Flintstone food group, that they ate every morning of vacation one summer until more and more of them remained uneaten each day. The unwanted pastel brontosauruses, when left in the milk more than a couple of minutes, grew like Chia Pets to three or four times their normal size and butted up against each other, forming a puffy psychedelic dome of sucrose film floating across the bowl. In a weak moment during cleanup one morning, I took a bite and, along with insulin shock, got some encouragement about the boys: even they had limits.

With preschoolers a year and a half apart, I again dismissed popular psychology and welcomed a bliss that fell over the house when I popped on the television at 3:30 in the afternoon. Just hearing the Sesame Street gang sing, "Sunny day . . . Sweeping the clouds away . . ." brought shrieks of excitement and wild anticipation. Cheston and Eric loved it too. In retrospect, a large portion of my sanity must have been on the line if thirty minutes of quiet had become that important. On one of those days at around 3:45, I had my first revelation about the limits of my influence. From the kitchen I heard Elmo the Muppet say a joke out in the living room, followed by a two-year-old Cheston laughing at it. In that moment it hit me that he was reacting to something without me. A stimulus from the culture (Elmo), not one originating from his parent, had manipulated Cheston's brain waves enough to prompt a shoulder shake and a giggle. The sudden awareness that he had his own funny bone reminded me that these little three-foot responsibilities were actually people who had not only a separate sense of humor but also their own full range of emotions that were not exactly like mine.

As the family expanded with the birth of Stephen, so did my allowance of TV time. One early evening the sound of crying floated up the stairs, which usually meant that one boy had hurt another boy. When I went down to see the damage, I found them all bawling over a show called *Rescue 911,* which was reenacting a story about a fireman who had a heart attack while driving the truck. I kept consoling them with, "Look, he's fine now. He's the one telling the story," but it took a while for them to calm down. A few years later, when Eric was about eleven, we watched Barbara Walters showing hidden camera footage of the abuse that older people receive in some bad nursing homes. After seeing an orderly beating an elderly man in a wheelchair, I was moved to tears and then looked over at Eric, who I thought would be bored, and saw him on the couch quietly crying too. He asked me, "Why are people so mean to each other?" After all the warnings about the dangers of cartoon evils, what was most frightening to them happened to and between real people.

Television aside, my "good parent" credentials could have been revoked over the matter of a couple of Italian plumbers. The Mario Brothers Nintendo game hit the market when Cheston was about eight years old, and he begged for one for weeks. I had no opinion about video games, but I had noticed that they had become a lightning rod in the network of naysaying parents, so I wondered what other mothers, the same ones who bragged about their feats of natural childbirth, would think of me. The rap on Mario was that he'd suck the creative juices out of a kid and turn him into a zombie, destroying his natural curiosity and making him a non-reading indoor dweller, level by level, life by life. So what was I supposed to do when my own electronically wired father surprised Cheston with a Nintendo at their house one evening? He even promised to come over the next day and hook it up. In Cheston's eight years I had never seen him flap his wings, his longstanding excitement indicator, so fast. He even flapped himself into a mysterious illness and had to stay home from school the next day.

I didn't really object to video games and television because to me it was just a sign of the times, and the times were the real issue. Once in a while I'd feel sad that my boys probably weren't going to be like Davy

Crockett and hunt their own dinner, wrestle bears in a vast pristine wilderness behind our homestead, and take to calling me "Maw" like real boys did. No matter that I extrapolated these unrealistic notions from TV shows like *Bonanza* or commercials for *Little House on the Prairie* since I didn't actually watch it because I never really related to pioneers or cowboys myself. Still, I came to idealize the rough and tumble life on the plains. I had to remind myself that I was raising my children in the 1990s and we lived in the suburbs for convenience, affordability, and a free public education. Still, the notion that the only good boyhood was one spent in nature—with no danger—was hard to knock even though we lived on a quarter-acre fenced lot and stared into the windows of our neighbors' houses on each side. So instead of fighting modernity, I capitulated to it and let the boys play video games until they "maxed out." My theory eventually worked. They lost the obsession with Nintendo and even television and as they grew older and more independent were out and about doing twentieth-century boy things like playing basketball, getting brain freeze off 7-Eleven Slurpees, and riding their bikes to the pool.

Yet in my insecure moments, usually born of comparison to other people, the list of noncompliance infractions of standardized, suburban methods and practices will whisper through my head. There was the whole music-lesson-inconsistency problem, miniature carrot deprivation, and the home haircuts that teachers were known to correct in class with scissors from their desk drawer, not to mention the glaring absence of Walt Disney World in their childhood. All the "should-haves" pale in comparison, though, to my angst over the charge to instruct one's children in the ways of God, the question posed at baptism to which we blithely answered "I will." But even Jesus knew that such instruction usually happens the other way around. It was Jesus, after all, who told the disciples not to hinder the kids from climbing all over him and that the kingdom of heaven belongs to "such as these." Once I loosened up in that area, I saw up close what he meant.

We tried to have family devotions on a regular basis, *de rigueur* in the spiritual circles in which we wandered. There was nothing I wanted more than to relay the love of God and the practice of prayer to my children, but it was the "regular" part that tripped me up. Every once in a while we corralled the three boys into the living room and opened up the Bible. It took but seconds for one of them to ruin the holy mood by making a funny face or a body noise which led to red-faced laughter stifling, all the while Fritz was trying to read a psalm or a parable. During other attempts our "family time" became like the old hockey joke, "I went to a fight, and a Bible study broke out." When it began to resemble a remake of Cain and Abel, we'd "mention" how love never fails in 1 Corinthians 13—or we would demonstrate the difficult concept of God's wrath.

Cheston did get the "love your neighbor (including blood relatives) as yourself" concept when I told him to split his heavenly Hardee's cinnamon-raisin biscuit with his brother. He thought a minute and said, "Mommy, I love Eric so much that I want him to have his very own." Eric also must have picked up a little theology along the way too. When they were at their height of cuteness, around four and five, I secretly watched them playing G. I. Joe outside. Cheston held out his man, running straight-armed in imaginary pursuit of Cobra Commander, the bad guy, and gave his surly command to "Pulvawize dem!" Little Eric took a different approach and tried to win Cobra's heart, following behind his brother screaming with evangelistic fervor, "Yeah, baptize dem!"

As noble as those living room catechism attempts were, the real lessons came in the dark catacombs of a bunk bed. I hadn't come across any how-to manuals on that phenomenon, but probably could have used one since Stephen began as early as age four asking the questions every parent fears at about the time the brain empties for the day. His fleshy cheeks, bowl haircut, and high voice belied the struggle he often underwent. "If God made the world, then who made God?" When my dad died, five-year-old Stephen was often distraught over what had happened to "Didi." "Where is he? Why do people have to die?" Some nights it seemed we had a little Jonathan Edwards in the house, he was so intense in his spirit.

In his early years, Stephen may have started out with numerology, announcing "Mom, I think in numbers," before demonstrating a speedy multi-digit multiplication "system" that left me amazed when I checked him on the calculator, but he always ended on a religious note. At bedtimes, when I was alert enough, I ventured what answers I could about these mysteries, offered little prayers for him—a practice which lasted for years— and did a lot of hugging. I knew even then how special and fleeting our conversations were. Those words spoken long ago so close together—this miniature Descartes and me—lingered in the air between us, sweet enough to be eaten like petit fours on a plate with two forks.

Innocence is good, but honesty is even better. One summer night between eighth and ninth grades Eric, who never had a problem voicing his displeasure, accused me of signing him up to help with the little kids at Vacation Bible School the next day without a signed affidavit granting his explicit permission. He let his frustration out at me from the top bunk as I moved in from the hallway, stood on my tiptoes, and hung my chin over the side. Once we worked out the misunderstanding about how he really didn't want to go, and how I said it would be a nice thing to do, and how it was too late, and how it was only three hours of an entire summer, he suddenly began to cry. This was one time as a mom I knew exactly what I had to do. I had to figure out how to get my forty-year-old rear up that narrow metal ladder and not whack my head on the ceiling so I could snuggle up to him. Once I made it, Vacation Bible School was the last thing on his mind. He really wanted to confess his remorse over losing his temper in some situations I had not even known about, and he was feeling sorry about it to the point of tears. Then he really opened up about feeling guilt over not having been very "faithful" to God, as he said, which meant not paying attention in church. On top of that he had been cutting up in Sunday school because he was bored since he was one of the few kids who didn't know all the answers in Bible Jeopardy. In essence he felt inadequate, but at the same time he didn't really care.

That was exactly how I had been feeling, which created a dilemma. Lying next to my middle son, staring at the plastic fluorescent stars stuck to the ceiling a few inches away, I faced a maternal moment of truth. Do I play the heavy and come down on him for misbehaving? Do I encourage him to try harder and do more activities to get close to God? Do I grill him about with whom and what he got angry? During that rare exchange, none of that seemed too important, and pursuing it would have come from my desire to protect my reputation as a mother. Right then, Eric didn't need a role model, a part for which I'd been a bit miscast in the past. He needed me.

But for the following part of the conversation, it appeared to be the other way around. His honesty about spiritual matters brought out my own questionings and before I knew it, my fourteen-year-old became *my* confessor. I told him how I'd been itchy too and was pondering the meaning of following God, which had begun to feel like a foot race that was hard for me to keep up in. Somehow in trying to nail down all the right answers I'd lost the whole purpose. It was strange but very freeing to let down my guard and speak from my own confused heart . . . to my son.

I was very sure about one thing, though, and told Eric in no uncertain terms. Over the years I had learned that several places in the Bible make it clear that God does not look at outer appearances, whether you're the five-time Bible Jeopardy champ or the loser who goes home without a single parting gift. No, God looks on the heart of a person, as only he can. Looking at Eric's distilled remorse, emptied of defensiveness, I have to believe that God would see what I did in the top bunk—a boy who was wrestling with his conscience and had ended up with a broken and contrite heart, the kind King David said that God would not despise.

That conversation was the end of my culture-induced parental anxiety and the beginning of a whole new tone and era in my relationship with the boys. From the time they were in my womb, the horror stories about the pain and dangers of raising kids in this world seeped into my heart, and fear made me want to defend them and dress them like G. I. Joes in combat gear. Then to make it to the big leagues of parenting, we were supposed to turn around and play offense, giving them endless experiences and skills early enough so as not to miss the chance to instill confidence and savvy, which of course portends a future of success. Either because they wouldn't cooperate or because I couldn't always toe the line, I let go on issues that in the end didn't make a difference anyway.

As Elmo's joke proved to me so long ago, they are not my clones or little projects to complete on someone else's timetable. I am amazed at how each one is finding his place and talents through a combination of experience, disposition, and the flow of grace in this life. As long as I live I'll never forget waiting at a stoplight while taking Stephen to school in eighth grade. He broke the morning silence with, "Mom, do you think we can find another piano teacher?" I squeaked out a "Sure." Then I could have spun my head around a few rotations when I heard, "Yeah, I think that when someone has a talent, they have a responsibility to use it." He actually used the word "responsibility." He had taken piano for a year way back in fifth grade, but his teacher became ill and he became disinterested. It took a while, but I found a teacher, and he's been at it a few months now, priding himself on "The Entertainer," which he can play cross-handed, or fast enough to sound like a record set on 78 speed, or as the ending flourish to every other song he plays.

All my worry about reading ended when Cheston's senior English teacher hooked him on British literature and changed his life. His sophomore year in college, I just about wet my pants driving him home for Thanksgiving when he looked straight ahead and blurted out from memory, "Shall I compare thee to a summer's day? / Thou art more lovely and more temperate: / Rough winds do shake the darling buds of May, / And summer's lease hath all too short a date," going on to recite Shakespeare's entire eighteenth sonnet to me. At home, as part of a personal challenge to read a book a week, he finished *The Grapes of Wrath,* and I heard him, at nineteen, crying on the couch. Though it was downright humiliating, I had to get him to remind me of its ending the way he does all the plots of books I've forgotten or never read. He went on from there at Christmas and finished *The Brothers Karamazov.*

Eric is finding his path too, developing his own way with words by working on the school newspaper, examining the status quo among his peers with occasional editorials, and delighting in notions of nonconformity. Every once in a while I can't help but think about their old friend Mario and how disappointed he must be. Now that I have a little perspective, I regret even a minute lost trying to develop a Polaroid of our bodies with other people's heads on them. And I see from these recent glimmers of maturity that there was no rush in those early days. These are unique and singular human beings with their own steady supply of creative juice.

And so am I, which is the very reason I struggled with not "doing" enough for them even though—for the record—we did a lot. From the beginning of motherhood until now, I craved time to myself in peace and quiet to pursue my singular interests or just get a good night's sleep so I could try. That desire to read or do art or be with my friends often felt like neglect of the kids, but I felt like a kid myself in many ways, just discovering my own place in the world. As my mother likes to say on this matter, perhaps for her own conscience, "more is caught than taught" with kids anyway. They tend to pick up on who we are more from what we do than what we say, since they haven't subjugated their intuition yet. But as much as I love them, I knew even then that the day was coming when they would go, and I wanted to maintain something of me for future use. To my surprise, that became the best thing I could give them after all.

The same *Grapes of Wrath* Thanksgiving, Cheston and I stood in the checkout line at the grocery store. In his wonderful, collegiate, full-of-himself naïveté he said, "I'm going to make my kids read good books." I had heard about these revisionist tendencies in adult children, the tendencies that make them overlook everything good you did and focus on the area they felt you failed them. My parental dander hit the roof. It was a holiday and a public place, so I refrained from striking him and calmly said, "Good luck. I tried a lot of things that you guys just refused to do." He flashed a touché grin, then wisely revised his observations. "I mean it's too bad kids don't take all their brain power, like we did to memorize every single fact about every one of our G. I. Joes, and apply it to something useful. You ought to be able to fill a kid's brain with great literature or teach him physics with how they are able to remember stuff." I paid the clerk, grabbed the cranberries, and said to him, "It's true. You really ought to."

ELEVEN

parenthood: a state
of full quiver

Like arrows in the hand of a warrior
 So are the sons of one's youth.
How blessed is the man whose quiver is full of them.

Psalm 127:4–5

As parents, we had gotten off pretty easily. There were the perfunctory broken bones and the gash over Stephen's eye from a brother "gently tapping" him into the edge of a table as they ran in to the public library for story time. (The blood and screams turned out to be much more entertaining than Curious George to the preschoolers there.) And as far as behavior, besides a teacher calling here and there about talkativeness and a few close calls when Cheston skateboarded, they had not been in any big trouble. Sometimes friends commented on how good they seemed, but I never claimed any credit because except for a belief that kids had a bottomless need for attention, my discipline strategy was very seat-of-the-pants. In fact, when it came to playing the heavy, I was a bit weak-willed. Not to say I was a pushover, just a little conflict-averse, which kids can sniff out like candy in your purse.

To get the boys to obey, especially when they were very little, I shamefully resorted most often to the bribery approach so I wouldn't have to carry out any of my empty threats of corporal punishment. When my brother-in-law got married, Cheston was four, Eric was three, and I was pregnant with Stephen. Eric sat to my left and when Cheston finished bearing the rings in his adorable mini-tuxedo, he filed in from the aisle on my right. That's the last I remember of Andy and Lauren's wedding. For the next forty-five minutes I was working deals on the front pew with a couple of three-foot high rollers. I spent the entire ceremony turning my neck right to left, shifting my big belly around, and whispering, "Okay guys, no talking. Stop. Please just sit still. All right, if you're good, after this is over we will go to the store and I'll buy you White Ninja or Sergeant Slaughter—any G. I. Joes you want. Okay, stop. Sit still." Then I'd switch to Mean Mommy and hold my index finger up to my lips and glare at them. Turning back to playmate Mom, I'd smile broadly, lean down to their level with bug eyes and whisper-sing, "A weel Amewican hee-wo . . . G. I. Joe!" I was exhausted before even getting to the reception.

I did have the advantage in these action figure negotiations since much of my postgraduate work involved rifling through hanging displays at Toys "R" Us, mumbling the name of the latest "hee-wo" like a gambler at the roulette table, "Come on, Dusty, Dusty, Dusty, gotta have a Dusty . . . ," desperately hoping to see his name on the upper right corner of the bubble pack. The whole time the boys watched me in intense silence from the shopping cart in their fat, puffy jackets. In those pre-school winters, this is where we'd go—a big indestruc-tible store—sometimes to shop but mostly just to kill time while I used my children as playthings.

In Kmart's accessories department, near the pocket-books and pantyhose, I'd discovered some huge, black, curly wigs. Soundproofed by sock-lined walls, I'd hide in the corner and dress up my fair-skinned, cheeky baby boys in an early Jackson Five look, then wrap scarves around their necks and hang pocketbooks off their shoulders. With that blank face that toddlers get when they are bone tired, surrounded by the big hair, they made me laugh so hard I feared some mean, apron-clad clerk might catch me and turn me in for something, like excruciating boredom. Consequently, even preschool-ers can figure out that the woman reduced to a heap of laughter in a corner of Kmart can't easily turn around and play the role of the heavy authoritarian figure very convincingly.

Thankfully, my Neville Chamberlain parenting tac-tics were balanced by Fritz's Winston Churchill style, but my tendency toward appeasement and ignorance would become a problem. Once they could drive and were no longer under my lame in-house control, my dis-cipline meant they had to call in during the evening, tell me where they were, and get home safely. Maybe I turned a blind eye to what was going on before they got home because I was operating in a vacuum, as though they were still innocent little boys hanging out with me at Toys "R" Us. All the while they had gained citizenship in a vast teenage kingdom of court jesters and village idiots who had those "personal myths" I'd learned about in college psychology—the ones that told them nothing bad could ever happen to *them*. My lifelong prudery, or ostrich-like stance, or both made me something of an idiot too, and I avoided broaching any subject of danger beyond driving. I held to my theory that kids need their parents' full attention, but as they grew older I failed to pay attention to reality. That was a big mistake.

It took almost nineteen years, but in a span of three hair-raising months we got wake-up calls for each son, and I was forced to yank my head out of the sand to answer them. It started when the oldest, Cheston, was a freshman in college and spring break loomed. He and his roommate got cheap airline tickets from Virginia to Florida and a free place to stay for part of the time they would spend there, in Panama City to be exact. My worries centered on safe travel and the money he didn't have to be doing this. Other people worried for me about what he was going to do once he got there. My normally unflappable seventy-eight-year-old mother got pretty flapped after happening upon an MTV (or was it the Wildlife Channel?) documentary about the incredibly debauched party habits of American college students, and the show culminated by highlighting the number one spot for these bacchanalia: Panama City. I brought all of this up, but Cheston assured us that he "knew what he was doing" and besides, it was his money and he was eighteen. That was supposed to both reassure me and render me powerless. The truth is, I had no reason not to trust him, and it is difficult to say "no" based on fear that something could happen.

Four days into the trip I got a phone call at eight in the morning. By then Cheston was in his cheap hotel room moaning to me about a severe stomachache. He had thrown up so much that he was becoming dehydrated. That began a day of phone calls between our doctors, the Days Inn, his roommate's cell phone, insurance companies, a doc-in-a-box in Panama City, and ultimately a community hospital. A couple of medical students in the ER took one look at the intense pain he was in and diagnosed him with pancreatitis, the inflammation of the pancreas. All the tests showed an outrageously severe case. Cheston's roommate told us the lead doctor said, "His parents are going to want to come down here." That did it. I was officially in a panic of the kind that makes you pace the floor, make travel arrangements and phone calls to relatives, and alternate between mumbling prayers and screaming them hysterically.

While our firstborn lay all alone eight hundred miles away in his room in a little three-story Florida hospital between a Burger King and a Target with a tube stuck in his neck and morphine coursing through his veins, Fritz started on the fourteen-hour trek through the cradle of the Civil War to get to him. I stayed home with the other two, which in a twisted way suited me better. As much as I may talk tough, I am not very brave. I didn't even have the courage to look up pancreatitis on the Internet for fear I'd see the word "death" near it. But having memorized the long distance number, I did talk to him several times a day. Not once did he remind me how old he was.

Over eight days, Cheston improved little by little, and on the last day Fritz asked the doctor in front of the boy what in the world causes pancreatitis. Without a millisecond of hesitation, he answered, "Excessive alcohol." Since it's pretty difficult to run when you have an IV tube in your neck, father and son had an afternoon in the hospital and many hours in the car the next day to discuss the matter and bond.

I heard the car engine that evening and ran to the front door. Although I knew he hadn't eaten solid food for close to two weeks, I wasn't prepared for the sight of Cheston. He'd lost twenty pounds off his tall and already skinny frame, and his auburn hair, which was college-long to begin with, stuck out like it belonged to a red-headed Einstein. His eyes popped from his blanched skin like two blue billiard balls in the snow. I hardly recognized him. For the next few days he recuperated at home, and as he got stronger, so did my anger. I grew more and more livid at how I'd been duped by the breezy charm he'd used to talk about college, telling me everything he knew I wanted to hear concerning his classes with a semi-sappy tone that would have made even Mister Rogers wince.

I was also angry with myself for wanting to stay in the world of childhood virtue and never confront or discuss the vices when innocence is lost. Late in the first semester Cheston had dropped plenty of hints about how he'd begun to appreciate one of Ireland's contributions to world culture in the form of a bottle of Guinness as a sort of shock test. I guess I failed, because his definition of normal seemed pretty normal and harmless to me. But once all the ounces of truth flowed out as medical information, I was uncontrollably aghast at the sheer volume of hops destroyed for his habit. I almost couldn't contain my sense of betrayal at being made to look so daft as a mother, whether I had it coming or not. Still a prude at heart, I was having a very hard time picturing my G.I. Joe baby in the kind of environments he described and wondered what good all my attention to him since birth, aimed at building self-esteem, had done for his sense of self-respect. As his pancreas got better, I felt like slapping him around with the dry toast he requested with his little weak-pancreas voice. Then one morning while he lay on the couch watching *The Price Is Right*, we had it out.

First I had one big, fat, ugly confession to make. Months earlier, as I cleaned up Cheston's room, I opened what looked like an old composition book and read the first two or three sentences. Written a few days after he'd graduated from high school, they described a wild senior beach week in June. It was as revelatory as it was prescient. At the time he told me things about the trip like how he and another kid sat on the beach, looked at the stars, talked about British lit, and reminisced about their great English teacher. I don't doubt that even now, but I have revised my mental picture from two little Alistair Cookes discussing Keats to two wasted Foster Brooks raising a couple and joking about their Grecian urns. I couldn't confront him without giving away my brief lack of judgment, plus I was in seriously stupid denial about what I had read.

My honesty about that old transgression first enraged him, but it wasn't just his physical leg that he couldn't stand on too well in that moment. I had him where I wanted him and calmly let out my disappointment over feeling fooled and like I was the kind of mother I had tried so hard to avoid being—the one you had to pull an Eddie Haskell on because she "wouldn't understand" or couldn't handle it. After that he knew he had better start pouring out the details of his social life like the beer at its source. He took responsibility but emphasized the rampancy of binge drinking at college and how he got swept up in the party mentality out of a compulsion I'd seen his whole life, the drive to "go do something."

We got out all the facts and history before the conversation turned emotional. I told Cheston that I had come across an e-mail his father had sent to a friend, asking him to cover teaching the senior high Sunday school class, saying, "My beloved son is in the hospital in Florida. I'm driving down there tomorrow." That did it for him, and he had to pull a pillow to his face. I moved from the computer desk to sit on the edge of the sofa, leaning over him like I'd wanted to during all those torturous phone calls to the hospital. That was when the real healing started for both of us.

That was March. The next wake-up call came in April from Eric at work.

"Mom, I'm sick. Will you come and get me?"

That was strange. He wasn't sick one hour before that when I dropped him off at the grocery store where he'd been a bag boy since turning sixteen a few months earlier. As I rounded the corner into the parking lot, he made the mistake of bounding out in his signature Groucho Marx stride with his arms stiff to his sides, wiggling his fingers.

"You don't look too sick to me," I said, as it became clear from his sheepish facial expression that something was wrong.

"You'll be getting a call from the assistant manager tomorrow." *Oh great.*

This local grocery store works very hard at maintaining an image of absolute perfection. The meat is pinky fresh, the floors so clean you could eat the sushi right off of them, and it seems that the employees, even the men, are required to smile like Miss America contestants. Therefore any hint of sexual harassment has to be nipped in the bud, so to speak. That is how I ended up in a part of the grocery store never seen or even considered by the average customer—the offices.

The assistant manager had quite a serious look on his face as he began to describe Eric's transgression. A young woman employee and Eric had been taking a break in the lounge *(Oh, God what's he going to say? Not a girl thing, please . . .)*, which was not a secluded area at all. *(Phew.)* The twenty-one-year-old made a suggestive comment to him, which was just one thing she was known for by every male in the store. Then he, my sweet, blonde boy, said something back that to this day he won't tell me, although he has characterized it as able to make Howard Stern blush. I still don't want to know. She actually laughed at being one-upped by this new guy and

130

made the mistake of relaying the conversation to another young woman who must have been working vice undercover in the deli. That person tattled on Eric and just like that the fear of a sexual harassment lawsuit hung in the air over both the store and Eric like the smell of four-day-old mackerel.

Before I could say anything, my imagination had a crew from *20/20* traipsing all over our house with cameras and lights, looking for plugs and interviewing Eric, whom they forced to repeat his ill-advised nasty remark. Then my reeling mind showed me a picture of our family sitting on a city sidewalk, shaking tin cups, holding a sign in front of us saying, "Wiped Out By Innuendo. Please Help." I mentally reentered the assistant manager's office in time to hear him say that they would issue Eric a warning and take him off the schedule for a week and that the girl did not show any inclination to sue. (She probably wanted Eric's number, though.) For the following week we waited for subpoenas and lawyers and nasty letters, but the legal part all passed, except for the private sentencing worked out with Judge Dad. Eric left his bag boy job, chastened about the trouble one's mouth can cause. I learned in front of a grocery store manager that my sixteen-year-old son actually knew more about sex than what his dad told him about the birds and the bees a few years back when I hoped he would take it as a science lesson.

The last wake-up call caught me completely by surprise with a knock on the front door. A lean, slow-talking policeman came looking for Stephen, our happy-go-lucky eighth grader. By then my maternal personal myth had ended so abruptly that nothing really surprised me, but still, this was my baby, whose every action I monitored closely not out of suspicion but out of even more paranoia about safety. I told the officer that Stephen was at a friend's house and asked what was the matter. He refused to tell me but said he would wait for me to go get him. *Whoa*. I got in the minivan and, resisting all urges to the contrary, drove slowly down the hill, quite aware that this policeman was watching me, to go find my youngest son. Looking in the rearview mirror at the uniformed officer on my lawn, I banged the steering wheel and asked God very loudly inside the car what I was supposed to be learning from all of this. What in the world could my fourteen-year-old, prepubescent, good-student comedian have done to summon a cop to our door? I found that very boy skateboarding in a cul-de-sac with a friend. He looked at me strangely since I was an hour and a half early.

"Stephen, Officer O'Brien is at home and wants to see you. What's going on?" I asked.

The way he looked at me went beyond "deer in the headlights," all the way to "Mafia hit." He has huge eyes anyway, and at the time they produced an inexplicable, involuntary reaction from his tear ducts that filled his eyes with water. I'd learned not necessarily to interpret the infilling as emotion, but at this moment that would have been right on the money. The trip back home was about five minutes, not much time to confess and repent and plead for mercy. All I got was that this might have something to do with a kid that he'd "played" with a couple of months ago. I remembered well dropping him off and picking him back up after a total of two hours after school. But that's all the time it takes, we'd soon painfully learn, to get into a fight with the law.

Once everyone was settled in the living room, Officer O'Brien confronted Stephen about his association with a boy we will here call Dick. The officer started to ask about that particular fateful afternoon but interrupted himself. Using a nickname for our son that no one else uses, he said in his slight drawl, "Now Steve, before I ask you any questions, I'm gonna have to read you your rights."

Wait a minute. Did he say, "Read you your rights?" As in Miranda? All of a sudden this went from a visit by Officer Friendly to a scene from *NYPD Blue.* I whirled around, turning my back to the man, and shook my head in disbelief so hard my cheeks reverberated. Fritz sat on the sofa next to Stephen, who was red-faced and speechless as Officer O'Brien went through the entire list of rights. My head was about to explode as I heard it all, starting with "You have the right to remain silent . . ." After being told that his case would be helped by cooperating, we let Stephen talk. He haltingly told how he and Dick had played football that day in the field of a nearby school. As it got dark they started back to Dick's house and when they passed a shed in the woods the kid got the idea to break into it and see what treasures it might hold. Stephen told us that he confronted the bigger boy, telling him not to do it, to which Dick replied that this particular school didn't need the stuff anyway. He grabbed as much as he could—just enough to qualify for grand larceny—then shoved a plastic bag of overflow balls at Stephen. When I picked him up later and asked my usual, "Did you have fun?" he answered looking straight ahead, "Yep."

Once it all came out we drilled into him the importance of coming forth, but we were also not so old that we couldn't remember the power of peer pressure. When this happened, the middle school alliances that Stephen faced had shifted and, unbeknownst to me, Dick emerged for a short time as a power player. He used his intimidation tactics to drag several other kids into his web, getting them caught for a little arson here and there, I found out much later. I had never had a good feeling about the kid, but in the extreme effort not to judge in my mind so as to be thought of as ever so nice, I ignored my gut for just the couple of weeks it took for Stephen to step into some deep trouble.

Officer O'Brien assured me that the prosecutor would deal with the boys separately and that we probably wouldn't even go to court. But Stephen still had to be booked—as in "Danno"—at the county courthouse. We met the policeman there, and I stood by the minivan and just about screamed and rent my clothes watching the squad car with my mop-haired kid in the backseat head to the county jail so he could be fingerprinted and get his mug shot taken. A mug shot! How was *that* going to play in Sunday school?

Most of the men around me talked about how all of this—as bad as it seemed—was a good way to learn a lesson. I maintained all along that Stephen was a victim of guilt by association, and that that was an injustice, not a lesson about failing to rat on someone. Stephen's only crime was being at the wrong place at the wrong time with the wrong person, and for that he had to be subjected to the same humiliation as Dick, who knew this routine well.

On the day of arraignment—another TV word I never thought I'd use in a sentence—we were told, contrary to everything prior, that every felony case had to go to trial. So when the day of judgment came, we arrived early with our lawyer, a longtime family friend, hoping to get a word with the prosecutor. We were beaten there by Dick's lawyer, who had gotten Dick a plea bargain on a reduced charge but never consulted us on how that would affect our case, as I naïvely expected her to. I really had been living in a cave somewhere, hoping I'd never have to confront anything or anyone. Court is one place where that is just not possible. We had only minutes to figure out if we should also take the plea bargain and accept guilt by association since simply carrying that plastic bag of stuff for fifty yards to Dick's backyard had incriminated Stephen. Or we could risk a trial on the more serious charge with a judge we had heard was by far the strictest. Against all my newfound sense of injustice, we took the plea.

Stephen bravely stood up and gave his apology, and due to that old tear duct thing, his statement was breaking my heart, but it did nothing for the judge, who seemed to lack one. A somewhat large woman about my age, she had wide-open eyes that not only revealed the entire circular pupil but had the disconcerting habit of looking off to the side as she talked to you. She made no sign that she heard my son before launching into a character-assaulting tirade, raising her voice and bugging out her eyes about his, or really Dick's, reprehensible behavior, telling him that there were "a bazillion" houses around that he could have run up to and called his mother to come get him. In a very undignified way she berated him, saying that he hadn't been in outer space so there were "a bazillion" places he could have escaped to, never mind that it was pitch black, a strange neighborhood, and these were save-face-at-all-costs middle schoolers. She seemed to think she was doing me a favor by repeating the phrase, "Your parents didn't raise you for you to . . ." in order to scare him.

She was wrong. It was all I could do to keep from showing her my real parenting approach by yelling something like, "Forbid it Almighty God, give me liberty or give me death!" and jumping over the bar in my pantyhose and straight black skirt to climb up the bench and grab her by the neck. Instead I sat in the front row of the gallery with one leg crossed over the other, moving it up and down like I was conducting Beethoven's Fifth with it, and glared at her. She ended her lecture by sentencing Stephen to exactly the same punishment as his corrupter, one hundred hours of community service, probation, and something called shoplifter's class. We joked (much later) about that being a course in which you first mastered the technique on penny candy, then advanced to small electronics before graduating to the finer points of hot-wiring. But it wasn't at all funny then. My closely guarded, nice-person reputation for pleasing and appeasing instantly vanished as I uttered a slight profanity to our lawyer once back out in the lobby.

What really brought me back to a sense of proportion over the whole thing was this friend's response. As we moved out to the parking lot, he reminded me of the experience early in his own life, when he too suffered from a misrepresentation of his character that ended up costing him a lifelong dream. I remembered the story well, and his honest and personal comment burst my self-pity and anger bubble. Then I started to feel ashamed of my suburban assumptions and overwrought sense of injustice in comparison to other communities where guilt by association is a way of life. While I, like most people, believe that to be unconscionable, I had not yet—not until sitting at the mercy of that judge—felt the injustice in *my* gut about *my* kid who was getting slapped around by a deaf and blind system. Suddenly the entire Dick affair became a lesson in compassion—ironically, because of a lawyer, but not just any lawyer.

Meanwhile the defendant had "quit ye like a man," as a magazine title that hung around our house for a while urged. Stephen had been much more patient and mature throughout the entire ordeal than his mother had. His debt to society would be paid over the last two weeks of the summer at a fairly kept-up nursing home nearby. We were both silent on the way over the first day, but I was much more nervous. When I returned at 5:00, I expected to see a bedraggled boy hanging his head. Instead he came skipping out of the front door and kicked his heels off the curb before spiraling into the front seat. "So . . . how was it?" came my routine question. Just as perfunctorily, he replied, "Fun." We possibly had a lemonade analogy coming out of this.

Besides the overwhelming smell of cleanser mixed with old people in his T-shirts, Stephen's stint at the nursing home gave him lots of new material. He has always had an eye for the comic and he needn't look too far in a place like that. After a couple of days, the maintenance men became his new "crew." They showed him how to use a drill, took him to Lowe's in the pickup truck to buy lumber, and generally let him do manly things outside with them. At lunch they watched HBO documentaries, discussed their many conspiracy theories about the government, and let Stephen in on some of the nursing home politics. After a few such talks, one older man revealed his chauvinism by saying, "You stick with us maintenance guys, boy, 'cause you ain't gonna git no 'ntelligent convasation hangin' roun' Housekeepin'." One night Stephen told how this same "old dude" cracked him up—maybe on purpose, maybe not—when Stephen asked, "Hey Bill, what time does your watch say?" He answered, "Sorry, son, this thing's battery-powered. It don't talk."

By the end of the first week I actually looked forward to what tidbit Stephen was going to bring home that night from either the maintenance guys or the residents. He told how he liked to roll the residents back from lunch down the linoleum hallways with enough speed to get what hair was left on the bug-eyed old ladies' heads to blow back like a dog's in a convertible. He talked a lot about one cranky old lady who stood in her doorway most of the day, smoking a cigarette and defending herself against imaginary accusers. Stephen swore that he would go up to Ticked-Off Lady, as he referred to her, screw up his face like hers, get up close, and teasingly ask why she was so upset. She'd reply with a crazed look, "I *did* love my Mumma and Daddy. You can't tell me I didn't love my Mumma and Daddy! You better love your Mumma, boy!" I guess I can thank her for that.

At dinner we listened to his imitation of Ticked-Off Lady's "conversations" with her neighbor, a very sweet lady born in Greece and raised in Nashville, whom Stephen nicknamed Tennessee Greek. Whether age brought it out or not, she still spoke her native tongue, only with a deep Southern accent. In his best gruff smoker's voice Stephen mimicked Ticked-Off Lady cursing and yelling at this sweet woman, then, quickly switching accents, he'd become an unfazed Tennessee Greek, pulling out what Greek he knew to drawl, "Well, I reckon it's a mighty fine spanakopita acropolis odysseus today, don't you think?" Then he'd end his routine with, "How dare you say I don't love my Mumma!"

By the end of the 100 hours, Stephen wondered if he might not get a community service sticker on his diploma for this experience. I told him that court-ordered service probably wouldn't count toward that distinction. But he still learned a lot of lessons that summer, among them how to cuss like a pro. But his mother learned a few too. Until that spring, I thought I had invested enough of myself in the boys to ensure their protection. I thought that by making our home a place where they could be themselves and myself into a mother who was fun and not simply an authority figure I could keep them talking and laughing so that other amusements wouldn't be so enticing. But they couldn't stay in a Kmart shopping cart their whole lives. Despite the fact that the handle warns, "Do not leave this child unattended," they grow up and go out into the world very unattended. Popular "parentspeak" would add "and when they do you just hope they draw on everything you taught them and make the right choices." But not all situations present themselves like the SAT, or even true-false questions, with unlimited time to think them over before filling in the bubble with a Number 2 pencil. That theory sounds good, but it doesn't always play out in human nature—sort of like hearing a sermon about loving thy neighbor, then losing it in the church parking lot when thy neighbor cuts you off.

Still, I blindly believed that through the sheer force of my personality my kids could resist, and possibly avoid altogether, having to make choices that included contact with the uglier sides of life and the uglier sides of people. Instead life came at all of us holding up a mirror, and it was time to face the truth. They were going to mess up. And if I kept ignoring or obscuring the earthier aspects of life for the sake of my own version of family paradise, then my children would be no more dimensional than their pictures in my wallet. By thinking good character simply meant doing nothing wrong, I had been living in a sentimentalized dream world that didn't teach the art of stepping up and dealing with trouble, especially trouble in the form of other humans.

Perhaps I had underestimated life's threats and didn't talk about them much because I'd been in the habit of assuming the kids to have parallel personalities to mine. When I was cold, I made them wear a coat. If I had not been tempted by something, then why should they be? If I grew up as a girl, then why couldn't they? But just because I was a priggish and analytical kid who carefully checked her every move didn't mean they wouldn't sign up for Mr. Experience's classes and learn by the mistakes on their tests. As difficult, painful, and sometimes frightening as it can be for a parent, kids (and adults) often don't learn what is right until a situation goes wrong and they feel that wooziness in their gut. They didn't appreciate me nearly as much when I was just dispensing Dramamine as when I held the vomit bag and stood by them until it was all better.

To a degree the boys' troubles were public and open to the world for reinterpretation of their character and my skills as a mother. Just as I took no credit when they were little, I took no blame when they turned into teenagers. And since that spring, I've marveled at the changes in some of their attitudes and habits as a result of those mishaps. The conventional wisdom taught me that children learn from ingrained habit and practice, the same way they learn the multiplication table. Now I tend to subscribe more to the idea of step growth, a calculus principle, where manhood is approached in giant steps with periods of leveling off in between. Every step is based on what each boy has seen with his own eyes, stirred around in his own head, and taken into his own heart.

Despite the rapid-fire heartache and headaches of those three months, now I am glad everything came out into the open. Love is love, but the kind that never fails shows up a little more when life turns a little ugly. It produces much better communication too. Before that spring our conversations had been a bit like those of Ticked-Off Lady and Tennessee Greek—in the same hallway but not in the same reality. Getting inside the boys' hearts more genuinely may be the very best outcome, and perhaps even an answer to the prayer I banged on the steering wheel that day.

TWELVE

the wedding banquet

He brought me to the banqueting house, and his banner over me was love.

Song of Solomon 2:4 KJV

Weddings are beautiful in a purposefully predictable way. It is the rare wedding that surprises us, where something totally unplanned happens. I'll never forget the one I attended during which the dad replied, "Her mother and I do," kissed his daughter, then tripped over the back of her dress, ripping the skirt from the bodice. This could not have been predicted. Likewise, I'll never forget the ceremony when something unplanned happened to me. I am normally all too composed when witnessing vows of holy matrimony, including my own, but that was not the case when the son of my friends Dave and Elizabeth Turner got married. This was a wedding in which not two but three families joined together, a father walked the aisle alone, and God's fingerprints were all over the guest book.

I met Elizabeth on the campus of the private school where our husbands both taught. I was recently married, a teacher, and pregnant with our first son. It was the early eighties, and Elizabeth was a high-powered woman working in the not-too-formerly man's world of advertising. Despite finding success there, she, like me, carried a well-disguised insecurity about her background not being "up to" those around her who might have had more worldly advantages growing up. In that shoulder-padded decade, she struggled with how much you really had to know versus how much you could just pretend to know in order to appear competent. Consequently Elizabeth, unlike me, tended to go all out in everything she did but was equally willing to drop everything when anyone needed her.

What really drew me to Elizabeth as a friend in those early days was her loud, hooty laugh. A person who laughed like that at my jokes was destined to be my friend for life. We both kept hooting through the birth of my three children, significant birthdays, countless diets, Glenn Close *Fatal Attraction* perms, stirrup pants, and enough female identity angst between us to make anyone's head explode. Married nearly a dozen years, Elizabeth had never been pregnant. Neither she nor Dave, an outrageously creative furniture maker and fine arts teacher, talked about having their own baby nor wondered too much about why it hadn't happened. But one Sunday in the mid-eighties, their indifference suddenly changed. Dave felt an overwhelming call during church to adopt, or as he put it, "rescue some kids."

Only a few weeks after putting their names into the system, the Turners had a home study done to prepare the way for a child who might need them. Instead they got two. Elizabeth called one day shortly afterwards and asked me to meet her at Burger King with my three boys. She had a couple of people she wanted us to meet.

We walked around to the side of the restaurant. There in a booth sat advertising queen Elizabeth and two dark-haired kids, all three wearing Burger King crowns. The girl looked about eight and the boy around ten. They were a brother and sister who had been severely neglected by parents who suffered from alcoholism and mental illness. They had spent not a few nights in cars and had bounced around in several foster homes. Despite the regal attire, John and Louise unceremoniously entered the Turners' home and hearts, and against all the loud woman-speak of the day, Elizabeth quit her high-powered job.

The road was not always easy with drastically reduced income, periodic threats from the children's birth mother to take them back, some inexplicable and manipulative behaviors, and later the normal challenges of raising teenagers. John and Louise appeared to embrace their lives in suburbia, loving the YMCA and youth group and eventually opening up their hearts to let their new parents inside. But the rescue effort could not reclaim those vital early years. Our friends spent untold time, money, and effort to get good counseling and suitable educational situations to give these two kids every possible advantage in the fast-paced, high-achieving part of town in which we lived—a world that threatened to eat them up.

After ten years of camping trips, Christmas pageants, summer camps, home schooling, private schooling, public schooling, birthday parties, and deep relationships with a vast extended family, following high school both children found their way back to their birth parents' town deep in the country. They kept in varying degrees of communication with the Turners, usually only calling when they were in trouble or needed money. But by the time the kids were both around twenty, the calls stopped altogether.

Elizabeth wondered if they had made any difference at all in the ten years John and Louise were in their home. She confessed to looking around at some of the "perfect" kids and families with a streak of envy and wondered why their kids had rejected and at times betrayed them. With the help of oceans of coffee, Elizabeth and I talked in countless restaurant booths about surrendering our expectations for children at a time when the whole society had raised the bar to impossible heights. My friend had given so much love to a stranger's little ones and rearranged her entire life, giving up the all-important decade of one's career—the thirties—in order to give them a chance in the world. I tried to remind her of the nobility of their efforts and that they were true to their call even if it didn't turn out the way she thought it should. But that was easy for me to say since I was raising three little boys who played soccer, did fine in school, and whose emotional baggage I recognized easily because it had name tags clearly labeled "Knapp." Despite all the praise and consolation they received during those years, the Turners couldn't help but feel a sense of rejection, and for Elizabeth a sense of failure, even though the kids—wherever they were—probably had nothing but warm thoughts for them. They simply couldn't ignore the pull of their kin or perhaps the familiarity of a decidedly non-suburban life.

Even during the later years with John and Louise, the pain in Dave and Elizabeth's hearts was not so great as to numb them. The "rescue call" came again—this time for a little seven-year-old string-bean baby doll named Valerie who had a wicked sense of humor and, much to Dave's delight, would quickly find her way around a band saw with great skill.

Elizabeth had gradually relinquished the older ones to God and learned how to protect herself emotionally from any lingering regret or rejection. By now she had thrown herself into the education of Valerie, whose ratio of energy to body weight was extremely high. Then one evening came a knock on the door. There stood John, now twenty-four, looking like a man to everyone else but a boy to them. He had grown tall, handsome, and serene, still twisting his mouth into a familiar, insouciant little grin. He came to tell Dave and Elizabeth how much he loved them, and he thanked them for showing him God's love and a good way to live. He also announced that he was in love and planning to get married.

The Turners soon met John's fiancée Amanda and saw what a good match she made for him, and the young couple became part of their lives. John and Amanda were planning to go to a local courthouse near her home to get married because her family really couldn't afford a wedding celebration and saw no practical purpose in it. But once Elizabeth and Dave learned that it really had been a dream of the couple to have a wedding, they offered to provide the two lovebirds with one. With extra money earned from the commissioned dining room set Dave made that summer and the piano lessons Elizabeth taught, they gave their son and his wife their dream.

Finally the big weekend in October arrived. At the rehearsal dinner, I noticed an unfamiliar man among Elizabeth's family. He clung to the edges of the room and spoke only to those who approached him, and even then with little more than a nod of the head and a polite but familiar grin. Someone then whispered to me that this was Mr. Ridge, Louise and John's birth father, about whom we had long ago heard some not-so-nice things.

He had a childlike shyness, the kind John still had too, and a handsome face with a Robert Redford quality to it. But this sharply cut profile had been worn and reddened by years of abuse. He averted his watery eyes often. In the years since John had left the two had reunited, and we learned that Mr. Ridge had gotten his life together and returned to the church. He brought a friend from his home church to the rehearsal dinner, a jolly, huge-bellied man with thick glasses who wore jeans and a T-shirt that boasted "Jesus Stomps Out Sin" with a graphic that resembled something from the World Wrestling Federation.

The bride's family seemed unaccustomed to social interaction and stuck to themselves, only grinning when spoken to even if asked a question. The father of the bride didn't come. The rehearsal dinner, though elegant and delicious, was subdued but not without its own quiet drama.

Sometimes the greatest payoffs in life come in a flash, a moment where an ending and beginning meet, sparked by knowing the histories of people who have been dear to us and have become part of our own stories through years of friendship. One of those flashes came during dessert after Dave Turner rose and toasted the bride and groom, then asked for any others who felt so inclined. I looked around at Elizabeth's four brothers as likely toasters, but heard the chair next to Dave's slide out from under the table. John's birth father stood up. The room became utterly silent. Instead of speaking to the couple, he looked right at our longtime friend Dave. With muffled words and a bowed head, Mr. Ridge said, "Mr. Turner, I want to thank you for what you done for my kids." I thought I detected his voice breaking a little. Mr. Ridge then reached out his arm, and the two fathers clasped hands.

The next day had its share of pre-wedding catastrophes and hurt feelings, but when the time came everyone was in place and the church was beautifully decorated. It was an especially bright day, which made the black-and-white floor tiles gleam and the high, light yellow walls wrap the room in warmth on that early fall day. Elizabeth chose purple and yellow roses for the flowers in the windows and along the aisle. The congregation ranged from Dave's nattily dressed colleagues from the most prestigious prep school in the city to others whose attire did not exactly bespeak a formal occasion. Some came in jeans and flannel shirts, and some wore polyester pants and flip-flops.

Elizabeth was escorted down the aisle by her father. She was seated, followed by the mother of the bride. The groomsmen and the best man, Dave, filed in place from a side door at the front of the church. We all readied ourselves to look back down the aisle at the processional, but one more person needed to find his place. Mr. Ridge stood with his hands folded in front of his body at the threshold of the church. In such a grand setting, this man who had nothing much to offer the world had everything to give back to his son that day by making that walk. As difficult as it must have been to feel all the eyes of the congregation boring into him, he walked down that long, royal red aisle with his lips held tight and eyes looking straight ahead. Many guests may not have even realized who he was. He took his place next to the woman who had been called to help raise his son, my friend Elizabeth.

The bridesmaids filed in wearing deep violet gowns specially made to fit all sizes and shapes. The organ began with Handel's Water Music as the bride and her father, who had just arrived an hour before, stood at the back of the church. He was a burly man with longish gray hair and big sideburns, and he wore a borrowed suit with pants that fit well below his belly and a white shirt unbuttoned enough to reveal his salt-and-pepper chest hair. Looking eager to get the whole affair over, he walked this daughter who he so obviously loved down

147

the long center aisle with his head down most of the way.

The service was beautiful. It included a reading by the young daughter of a close friend who had just come through terrible cancer surgery and a song offered by a young sister-in-law who had recently been diagnosed with multiple sclerosis. Like many weddings, it included a time to light candles symbolizing the two families joining together. The bride's parents lit the first one, followed by Elizabeth and Dave. But before John and Amanda went up, the minister nodded to the other person sitting in the front row. John's father stood up, made his way to the chancel, and lit his candle.

My assignment was to circulate through the reception and take photos of everything from the tiramisu cake sprinkled with rose petals to the fruit topiaries to the crusty baked brie to the shrimp dip. I took a few of the people too. The bride and groom fed each other cake, toasted their nonalcoholic punch to each other, and glowed. They never thought they could have a wedding. I don't think Amanda, coming from her modest background, ever could have imagined the beauty that Elizabeth and Dave had planned and orchestrated for her. John and Amanda would have gone to a judge and simply made their marriage legal. But it was the parents' nature to give. This small but elegant affair on a fall afternoon in a church fellowship hall was perhaps a little awkward, but it defined and celebrated a love that defied convention and was all the more powerful because of it.

The following Monday Elizabeth showed up at my door. Unlike Saturday afternoon, the day was overcast. Everything seemed particularly quiet that morning. I started blabbing on and on about the wedding, starting with that wheel of baked nut- and jelly-topped brie. She interrupted and shocked me with the confession that she had been deeply disappointed with so much of the day. Different personalities had conflicted with hers, and others had been rude to some of the staff at the church, which the Turners no longer attended, causing heightened tension. Someone, in a severe lapse of couth, shared with Elizabeth some unflattering rumors about some of the guests—rumors that turned out to be completely untrue. The postnuptial letdown combined with replaying all these run-ins was souring the entire experience for Elizabeth. Those old insecurities about presenting the proper image and carrying events off in a sophisticated manner crept in to stir up shame and mix up priorities. She worried about "what people would think."

As a friend, I knew what I had to do. I had to give her a *Moonstruck* Cher-slap of sorts. I verbally whapped dear Elizabeth across the face with a "Snap out of it!" She needed some perspective on the whole day and possibly on her life. It is precisely for moments like those that we need to have a history with people. As Elizabeth sat uncharacteristically sheepishly in my faded pink wing chair, I browbeat her with comments my mouth generated like a thesis outline. First I hit her with the snotty "if they are your real friends," then moved to reminders of the original call to rescue some kids, and ended with how much I personally cried at the wedding even though I couldn't yet explain why.

She was grateful for the priority check and left after both of us got over the seriousness and hooted about something or other. I closed the door and wished I'd said something else. The words weren't quite in order or available to neatly sum up all I'd witnessed the Turners do to give those kids a "normal" life and to love them as their own, up to and including the gift of that wedding. All I knew was that I couldn't have done it. I could analyze and extol, but my heart had been cold, a bit of a whitewashed tomb, until that wedding helped me see out of it, into the sunlight.

After all those years of sacrifice, the Turners had been rejected by the children they had adopted and promised to rescue. That was not in the plan. When all was forgiven, Elizabeth and Dave wanted to show their love in a beautiful wedding that the bride could never have imagined. This is love that contains seeds of the divine. Likewise my own insecurities, although covered with middle-class small talk and matching clothes, were mirrored in the look on John's father's face, a look of unworthiness. Yet he walked that long, unfamiliar path from the threshold into a glorious event. Perhaps I cried like a baby at that moment because deep, deep down God was reminding me of a heavenly banquet and some kind of unfamiliar beauty that awaits us, all the walking wounded, unaware and undeserved. Although for the side of the church I was sitting on that day the need for a benefactor may not have been so apparent, the need is there. Everyone is afraid and everyone to some degree feels ashamed. But there is an open invitation to the feast.

Because I was taking pictures during the reception I looked closely at John and saw a happy young man surrounded by his fathers' love. He was a far cry from the little boy I met wearing a Burger King crown. In his tuxedo, he stood as a dapper example of the royal grace it takes to raise a child, any child. That's what I wished I had told Elizabeth.

grace
THROUGH THE DAILY GRIND

THIRTEEN

thrifty . . . and brave

Do not worry about your life, what you will eat or drink
. . . Is not life more important than food?

Matthew 6:25

In everything, do to others what you would have them
do to you.

Matthew 7:12

I suppose the grocery store is an unlikely place to con-
sider Jesus' question of who my neighbor is and how I
am to treat him, but over the years I've been put to the
test there. Add discount meat into the equation and I
find it very difficult to resist the "every man for himself"
counterargument and fail the moral quiz. Back in the
late eighties, when eating was much simpler, another
mother told me that a different store than the one I normally patronized actually put food on sale when it

reached its "sell by" date. This high-quality, family-owned grocery store took packages of hamburger, chicken, and fish and slapped on a big, red, zigzag-edged sticker that said "THRIFT MERCHANDISE: 50 percent Will Be Taken Off at the Register" even though everything was still perfectly good. All you had to do was pop it in the freezer once you got home. The other thing you had to do was get there on either a Tuesday or Thursday right as they opened at 8:00 in the morning. The thrift only lasted an hour. As my friend relayed this top secret information, I had to blink my eyes hard to make them work again, *and* I had to swear to keep this to myself.

At the time, this news came like manna from heaven. Besides already being an avid and accomplished bargain monger for nonperishables, I wasn't working a regular job after our third son Stephen was born, so being able to get such a savings on the most expensive food group—meat—went a long way toward ensuring my peace of mind. When Tuesday came around I waved good-bye to the older two boys at the school bus stop before Stephen and I drag raced the two miles to the store to get there by 8:00. Squealing tires and spinning into the parking lot, my old red minivan pointed directly at what looked more like the turnstiles of Disney's Space Mountain ride in August than a food market. Obviously the secret had gotten out. Meat-minded customers, split between white-haired retirees and mothers with young kids like me, lined the sidewalk starting at the automatic door. I yanked Stephen out of his car seat, grabbed his hand, and pulled him along so quickly that he looked like a three-year-old walking on the moon.

Like they were counting down for a rocket blast, the anxious shoppers checked their watches as the big hand drew closer and closer to the top of the hour. Precisely at 8:00 A.M., the manager came to the other side of the

154

automatic door, unlocked it, and, keeping his arms and body fully protected, slid it open. Before I knew it, Stephen and I were caught up in something akin to a rock concert or, considering the majority of the crowd, a taping of Lawrence Welk. Instead of rushing a stage, we were flowing in one steady stream toward a little cove area to the right that was labeled overhead "Choice Meats." Still dragging poor little Stephen in his big coat and pom-pom hat, I followed the pack, now in full canter. On the way in I keenly noticed that a few old men and ladies, probably thrift veterans, didn't even take the time to get a basket. So neither did I.

We ended up circled around an inconspicuous, refrigerated case as I tried to get my breathing under control. Since I had been near the end of the line running in, I was on the outer ring of what looked like ice fishermen surrounding a hole in a frozen pond. My strategy to get at the red-dotted packages from this disadvantaged position was to summon as much Southern charm as possible while elbowing my way in like the best of them at Filene's Basement. Without grabbing, I either tip-toed to reach over the inner circle's shoulders or bent my knees in order to stick my hand through the triangular underarm spaces of the old people's bodies as they reached forward into the meat case. After extracting ground sirloin, pork chops, and catfish, I was having a hard time balancing them in the crook of my elbow, which was why having a toddler along was a big help for once. As my baby stood behind the ring of hovering adults, looking much more mature than we did, I handed him a load and said, "Here, Stephen honey, hold this ribeye and pack of thighs. Mom's going back in to get some breasts."

After everything had been picked over, I felt like I had stormed the Bastille and gone on to loot and pillage the nobles in the French countryside. Putting the booty away at home, I realized just how much I love not paying full price for anything. Now that that included pork chops, life seemed to have limitless possibilities. Once I had tucked close to two weeks' worth of dinner foundations away in the freezer I made myself a cup of cocoa to celebrate and think about what I'd do differently next time, especially to avoid being stuck on the outer ring. I also couldn't help but call my friend Catherine and tell her what had just happened to me, even though that was breaking code.

The following Thursday we arrived as early as we could to beat the white-haired crowd and were met by a big pink sign taped to the inside of the glass front doors. At first it made me fear that this windfall would end the way most that are too good to be true do—right after I find out about them. Instead, like rules at the swimming pool, the sign warned: "Due to the unfortunate number of injuries that have occurred as a result of the thrift hour, we ask that you be considerate of others and refrain from any running or pushing. If restraint cannot be exercised, we will have to discontinue the thrift." Catherine and I looked at each other with the exact same hooting impulse to stifle. I was glad we did, too, upon hearing a voice in the crowd say, "I heard last week a young lady fell (while everyone in line was thinking "or was she tripped?") and broke her arm." In the weeks following, the store began letting small groups of people in at a time to cut down on markdown violence, making it even more important to get in line early.

My satisfaction with getting half-price staples overpowered any shame or loss of self-respect I may have felt at being so obsessed with beating others to the punch to get what seemed like free food. But months later, after the thrift had been woven into my lifestyle, even I had the limits of my grubbiness tested. I saw Catherine by chance at the store just doing some normal anaerobic shopping a good thirty minutes after the red stickers were all gone for that particular day. We were talking side by side while we waited to pay until we noticed that the lines weren't moving at all. The manager came to my checkout and, after poking at the cash register for a few minutes, made an announcement that made me want to look around for Allen Funt. Very calmly he said, "Ladies and gentlemen, may I have your attention. We seem to be having some problems with our computers here. They're not reading the bar codes. So until we can get them fixed, we are going to have to charge you 75 cents for each item in your cart."

Catherine and I looked at each other like Lucy and Ethel and did not have to say a word to know the other's thoughts. She and her cart stood at the back of the line beside me, still free to roam. I was trapped up close to the end of the conveyor belt in front of several people and would be forced to unload and check out when the man in front of me finished. So with no time to waste, Catherine tilted her head and rolled her eyes towards the rows of food behind us and silently mouthed to me, "Whad-da-ya want?" Wondering—but not caring—if I weren't Exhibit A in some college kid's psychology experiment, I turned my back completely to the checker. From that vast 75-cent emporium, all I could think to mouth back to her was "milk." She nodded in acknowledgment and, being careful not to draw the slightest bit of attention to herself, slowly peeled away from her basket. In seconds she returned just as nonchalantly with my cheap milk. By now it was my turn to check out, and when I looked back from the conveyor belt, I saw Catherine's back to me as she disappeared into the cereal aisle.

Later, my ethics in that situation bothered me. I didn't think I would be so quick to capitalize on another's misfortune and work it to my advantage, but with no thought I exempted the faceless store from my do-unto-others list just as I had the other folks in line on the side-

157

walk waiting for the thrift. Theoretically, the others on the sidewalk are not my fellow combatants but my "neighbors," the ones that I am to love as myself. Yet that may take just a bit more goodness than I am capable of summoning, especially where groceries are concerned. The important thing was, like the pink sign told us, to at least refrain from being pushy to the point of harming others.

Ever since this same family-owned, high-quality grocer opened a new store in the shopping center at the corner near me, it has affected my life like taking a lover, only one the other men in the house would welcome. I spend way too much time there—so much so that I refer to it as *my* store. Plus it is full of temptation. This is no little Acme or Piggly Wiggly. Once in a while I'll waltz in to find a camera crew filming the cabbage or pot pies and a smiley girl interviewing the sous-chef for a spot on a national business channel. This store has wooden floors under the produce area, chandeliers, and a café with a yogurt bar, gourmet coffees, chi-chi sandwiches, and a sushi bar. But the upscale look doesn't mean uptight employees. The woman behind the deli counter always slices my lunch meat with a smile, even when I rush up at 10:00 when the store is about to close. I love to hear her say "thank you, baby" as she sends me on my way with my pastrami. It's no wonder this chain has a total lock on the city's grocery dollars.

Completing this store's perfection was its very own thrift hour, but the whole concept was fast losing its edge. One of the last exciting runs would also be a pathetic example of the fine line we all walk between our minds and our stomachs. As I drove up one morning, I saw my friend Pat already in line on the sidewalk. She is a writer, so after we both exclaimed how wonderful this new grocery store was, I started picking her brain for free writing advice like I always do. We began a fairly deep literary conversation as the manager opened the sliding glass door. This petite, more-Southern-than-I college professor interrupted herself and said, "Grab a little hand basket by the apples on your way to the back." I looked at her hard and thought, "Wow. Good advice. That will be fast *and* eliminate the elbow-crooking problem." Pat and I were still discussing a great book she had been reading as we graduated from walking, to trotting, to full canter in lock step across the spotless wooden floor, winding our way through the fancy produce carts and beating our fellow shoppers to the cases in the back. By then we had stopped our intellectual conversation altogether and stood silently beside each other rifling through the red-stickered packages.

Soon enough, though, as a B. B. King/Bob Dylan collaboration might say, the thrill was gone because the times they were a-changin'. My run with Pat came somewhere at the end of 1995 or beginning of 1996, just before the stock market skyrocketed, I'm told. Perhaps in direct proportion, expensive gourmet foods began to outnumber the basic things on the shelves, and—because of the trickle-down theory—also created sort of an Age of Aquarius Thrift. Now opening at 7:00 A.M., the sale lasted for three hours every single day, and the red stickers polka-dotted much more than just boring old meat inside of two huge, twenty-foot cases. It soon became difficult to find the chicken parts or cube steak in the midst of the dozens of sturdy plastic containers full of international and gourmet dishes that even at 50 percent off were still outrageously priced—irresistibly delicious, but outrageous nonetheless. Everything from tortellini Florentine to Mediterranean seafood pasta to tarragon chicken salad, foods that once were restaurant-style fare, became rather ho-hum. Then there were the racks of pecan pies, cheese biscuits, and mini-croissants, all half off too.

With so much supply and a longer time frame to shop, the demand for the discount dropped off dramatically. You never saw a line on the sidewalk at 6:45 anymore. No, no one seemed too concerned with getting bargain natural grain bagels—no one except me, out of my ingrained habit of looking for a deal. However, as I had gotten older, I rather enjoyed the calmer atmosphere, more often than not having the entire discounted offerings section completely to myself to browse at my leisure. But one day neither the thrift area nor I was so calm.

It's important to note that this grocery store stands on the county side of an intersection that forms a border with the city. Several times a day, buses from all over make a stop at that crossroads on their way to the mall a mile farther west before heading back east into the city. From my car I often see some of the familiar faces of the grocery workers sitting on the long brick wall in front of the dry cleaners, waiting to go home.

That particular morning I entered the store and was just meandering toward the thrift section when I noticed from afar an unusual number of shoppers. It was actually kind of exciting and nostalgic so I picked up my pace. As I shimmied my way in around the low refrigerated cases, I noticed a young, blonde woman whom I'd recently met at the kids' school standing beside me with her baby in the cart off to the side. Jazzed by the old buzz in the air, I sidled up to her, said hello, and just to make conversation commented, "Wow, it's kind of busy in here today." She nodded at the crowd rummaging through the goodies and pulled her chin over her left shoulder to me. Speaking out of a dragged-down corner of her mouth, she quietly said, "Yeah, it's all the white trash that gets off the bus."

I imagine this girl was probably cheering at a pep rally when Catherine and I were scrounging up discount food and trying to squeeze a little cow out of our budgets those many years ago. If I had been Madame Defarge storming the Bastille then, she was like Marie Antoinette. She seemed to resent that other people—not in her world or realm of experience—needed to eat too. Did only certain zip codes get a shot at the twentieth century's version of "cake," probably something more like balsamic tabouli, that day? Her protectiveness could be understood, but maybe not forgiven, if we were fighting over bread or a chicken for our pot, but we were rifling through sturdy containers hoping to get that heavenly tarragon chicken salad with the little white raisins for a mere $3.69 a pound.

Her comment also violated the rules of fair play established for the thrift and really should have garnered her a technical foul. There of all places there should be no gate passes required since the thrift is a 50 percent off gift from the management made available to the customers before donating the rest to charity. Everyone who is able should be allowed to elbow their way around the common refrigerated trough and do the best they can with whatever means they bring with them. I should know. I was the Mark Spitz of the thrift.

But she didn't know that, which made me wonder why she would make that comment to *me*. Did something about me create a sense of like-mindedness that made her feel safe? The sad thing was that I didn't do anything to change whatever perceptions she may have had either. Because of longstanding spinelessness issues, I didn't say anything and just moved away. Still it galled me that this young mother did not know me at all on the inside but only from a social context that put me in a category with her. She didn't know my history, much less my inherited and highly cultivated methods of finding bargains regardless of the cost to my self-respect. That she would see me as someone who would be sympathetic to her derisiveness made me wonder if I had subconsciously tried too hard to project an image of being at the height of respectability but only paying half price on my way up.

It is easier on the conscience and ego not to take a good look into other people's faces and see commonality or, stretching a bit, even brotherhood, especially when you perceive yourself to be in some battle with them over limited poultry or, worse, stratified social status. But just as I was convicting her of high crimes in my mind, the tables were turned. Because I am hopelessly double-jointed, the finger I had been pointing at her bent back around and nailed me in my little self-righteous heart.

The very day I finished recounting on paper this infraction of grocery store etiquette I set out to get my hair cut. Waiting to pull out onto the main drag heading west, I saw a woman in a grocery store uniform walking in the rain on a bone-chilling December day and realized that it was the cheerful woman from the deli counter. Since she had been on my mind, I felt this might be one of those little divine appointments, and indeed it turned out that way, only God didn't give me a lollipop afterwards.

I whipped onto the side street and as she approached the window, looking suspicious, I said, "Hi, you wait on me at the deli all the time. You want a ride? It is so cold." Once comfortable, she said it: "Well thank you, baby." I asked her where she needed to go, but only heard that she had a few minutes before her kids came home from school. She pointed to a street on the right only a half mile from where I picked her up and only twice that distance from my house. Still confused over where we were headed, I asked, "Are you going to see a friend?" To my surprise, she said "Oh no, here is my house right here."

She hopped out in the cold rain thanking me more, and I told her I'd see her at the deli soon enough.

Driving off, I felt a little woozy. Why would my last thought and not my first be that she lived so close by? Was it that she didn't have a car, or that she worked at "my" grocery store? It was wrong of me. I hoped she hadn't caught it or taken offense at my stupid insinuation. Though my question was not as openly crass as that young mother's jab and didn't impugn her character, on the inside I had made a judgment about her status based on a few misinterpreted outward factors.

As disappointed as I was with myself, that divine encounter pruned away some debris so I could see what common ground I shared with this person, without being separated by the two sides of the deli counter. When I saw her walking, I assumed she was out on such a raw day because she had missed the bus, yet once in the car she volunteered that she liked to walk to get her exercise. I told her that I often walk to the store for that very reason. We were women of the same age, with kids at the same school who were both working to help raise our families. Regardless of class, income levels, neighborhood, race, or even whether you buy retail or thrift, we all need to eat.

Food is the universal creaturely need and getting it the common pursuit. That need for sustenance, not to mention the other more spiritual human needs, should unite people in common experience. Instead, so often out of fear of getting our first hunger pang, we become combatants. Whenever there is a perceived sense of shortage, whether of edible goods or the more elusive commodity of self-worth, a switch flicks on out of a deep-seated worry that either we won't get our fair share or we won't measure up, or worst of all that we will appear lacking. We can end up in a race in which we look straight ahead and don't really see each other except

163

as a faceless adversary to push and shove out of the way to get first dibs.

An old prayer I've heard twice now at weddings asks God on behalf of the new couple "to help them in their struggle for bread." I wonder if that includes a nice piece of salmon if you remember to ask God out on the sidewalk to miraculously open up a spot around the refrigerated case right near the fish. I doubt it. In our struggle for bread, either fresh or day-old, we are supposed to remember the birds of the air that neither sow nor reap nor store away in Reynolds Wrap in the freezer. It may be that we are programmed to operate in our own best interest, and shamefully do so especially in times of abundance. Yet with an assurance that each day will have enough grace for our spirits and food for our stomachs, how much easier it is not to discount, but to actually value, other human beings in the same struggle.

FOURTEEN

st. christopher's revenge

For God has not given us a spirit of fear, but of power and of love and of a sound mind.

2 Timothy 1:7 NKJV

During my junior year in high school I bought my first car, a misty blue 1965 Volkswagen that sported a crank sunroof and a working radio. It only cost two hundred bucks, so the contrasting black replacement fender on the passenger side didn't bother me. With its headlights on, the car looked like the dog with the black ring around its eye on my favorite after-school rerun show, *Our Gang*, so I did a girly teenage thing and nicknamed it Petey. With my friends cramming their heads out of the open sunroof, hooting and hollering to passersby, we carried on the tradition of the people's car.

The only problem with Petey was his occasional disinterest in starting. One early spring morning I rushed out for school and learned that a motor, like a disobedient dog, won't always roll over on command. My mother clued me in to a little secret about manual transmissions she'd learned from her old Bel Air. If the car gets up enough speed the driver can depress the clutch, shift into second gear, pop the clutch, and the car should start right up. Fortunately, we lived at the top of the best sledding hill for miles around, so on that drizzly morning we tried it.

Like lining up for a soapbox derby, Mom pushed Petey into the street. Sitting in the car, I grinned and yelled my favorite Spanky quote out the window to her, "I don't know where I'm goin', but I'm on my way." As my VW headed down the big hill, an eerie silence filled the interior of the car. This must be what parachutists feel right before they pull the ripcord. All I heard was the sound of the little narrow tires whirring along the road, and when it seemed my speed was sufficient, I did what I was told. I pressed in the clutch and shifted into second—but nothing happened. The steep hill was quickly flattening and sweat was breaking out on my forehead. *"Mom, nothing's happening!"* I yelled. But it was like telling another driver to "go ahead"—out loud—inside your car. She couldn't hear me, but my deafening screams reverberated throughout the rounded cab. I glanced quickly in the rearview mirror and saw a gray-haired woman in a flannel nightgown and raincoat jumping up and down, yelling something back at me.

I had whirred almost to the bottom of the hill and the only audible engine noise came from a real car barreling down on me. I waved for him to go around, still pushing and popping to beat the band, and looked in the rearview mirror one more time. Mom was twisting her right wrist over and over again like a mime trying to start a car. Oops. Turning on the car was the one thing she'd forgotten to tell me, assuming I would know such a technical detail. By now the car was barely rolling, so I quickly arched my legs against the floorboards, reached into my bell-bottoms, grabbed the key, shoved it into the dash, and once again threw Petey into second gear. Only now I'd turned a corner and come to a dead stop. Thoroughly exhausted, I laid my head on the cold steering wheel. Then a noise like the car had eaten one too many burritos came from its rear end. I raised my head and, lo and behold, that small poot strengthened into a volks-Wagnerian engine ring. With neither the clutch nor me now depressed, I zipped around the block back toward Mom, who had lost sight of me for those few dejected minutes, to show her that her little trick and her little daughter got the car going.

That incident was well before my serious car anxiety began. And while it is difficult if not impossible to pinpoint when a neurosis begins, the seed of my biggest one must have been planted shortly after we sold Petey, which was ten years later, well into the first years of marriage. I actually made a profit, easily getting the $500 I advertised. A rough-looking guy smelling of whiskey came to buy it and asked us, "How do you spell that word 'hunderd?'" Fritz and I were so tempted to say, "t-h-o-u-s-a-n-d," but our consciences prevailed. I had really loved that car. It represented my youth and independence. Its peculiarities, rather than being maddening, made it more fun, and despite its occasional breakdowns, I trusted it. But that security came from the ignorance of that same youth. As I grew older, an inexplicable transportation fear made it harder and harder to ever again feel carefree toward a car or independence.

Among the reasons we had to sell the Volkswagen was its lack of baby Fahrfenugen. Plus, when we became parents in 1982 we thought it would be a bit irresponsible to cart around an infant in a vehicle made in 1965. So we bought a 1966 Volvo. That Swedish bombshell, a

122S sedan (still my all-time favorite car despite its numerous betrayals), always started. It just wouldn't turn off. The key, a huge round head with a skinny little shaft, had the habit of breaking off in the ignition—with the engine running. That Volvo set the stage for a whole cavalcade of family automobiles that emphasized "estimated" over "time of arrival." We still had Fritz's rotting 1972 Datsun 510 wagon from college. It would have been fine if we had engine trouble with that car since we could have just stuck our feet through the rusted-out floorboards like the Flintstones and run for help. We had to keep our tetanus shots up to date, though. The 510 got deep-sixed after it had fully entered menopause, overheating at the most inconvenient times, like when I was on my way to school where thirty students, most with criminal records, waited for me.

With a second kid coming along, we finally bit the bullet and traded up. I'll never forget staring out of the bay window of our first rental house and seeing Fritz jump out excitedly from a soft yellow, seven-year-old Audi Fox wagon. But it soon became painfully clear that we were the ones who got foxed. It was always something; if the rack didn't get us the pinion would. As my father used to say, you could just look at that car cross-eyed and it would blow a head gasket or crank its shaft or something mechanical. (I caught the tail end of NPR's *Car Talk* radio show recently when a woman called in about her Audi Fox. She barely got the car's name out of her mouth before the advice-giving brothers broke into merciless, wind-sucking, sustained laughter.)

Our transportation woes really showed up on long trips. If country inns on the byways of America brag "George Washington slept here," then markers along Interstate 95 could boast "the Knapp family broke down here." The granddaddy of them all came in the Volvo one Christmas Eve. Fritz, his two brothers, and I headed up I-95 to visit my in-laws in Connecticut for the holidays. Along about exit 13 on the Jersey Turnpike, just as it was getting dark, the right front wheel began moaning and grinding as if it were having a cavity filled. We limped off one of those high, arching ramps into the town of Rahway. Having been a pretty sheltered Southern girl, just the name New Jersey was threatening. Then I remembered where I'd heard the name Rahway. It was the site of a prison documentary I saw on PBS called "Scared Straight," the one where scary-looking prisoners curse virulently at juvenile offenders to deter them from a life of crime. When we rolled off the ramp, that very prison loomed over us before we ground into an empty Exxon station.

On the window of the locked office next to the Christmas wreath hung a sign saying, "24-Hour Towing and Service. Call anytime." What luck! Fritz dialed the number from a pay phone in the parking lot while the rest of us stood up against the glass office door. My brothers-in-law and I thought it was strange that we could hear the ringing so far away until we realized it was coming from the phone inside the deserted gas station. We sat on the curb on that Christmas Eve in Jersey wondering what to do next. In no more than ten minutes, a guy named Joe miraculously drove up in his wrecker, wiping his turkey dinner from his beard. He hopped out in front of us and in that beautiful New Jersey dialect said, "Yo, you'se guys got a problem witcha car?" His pager had gone off at home so he left his Christmas dinner to help us. I never again associated Rahway with bad people.

Other breakdowns came in a '78 Chevy wagon near Petersburg—right *in* the tollbooth as that scene from *The Godfather* played in my mind. For a while Fritz drove my dad's old Pontiac Brougham, an impeccably maintained, monstrously outdated, twenty-year-old, fat cat car with a quarter of a million miles under its fan belt and a grille that looked like it could turn into a giant set of teeth and eat large animals. When my trusting husband used it for a business trip, it was not uncommon to get a phone call something like this: "Come pick me up at Shoney's. The car's in Fredericksburg. I hitchhiked." At Shoney's I would find him dressed in his business suit, sitting on the curb, holding his head in his hands, and I'd try to picture my preppy-looking hubby walking backwards along I-95 with his thumb up.

My nerves, like our cars, were just waiting to break down over our sordid vehicular past. My guess is that kids had something to do with my growing anxiety. Lugging them up and down Interstate 95 to visit my in-laws in Connecticut may have triggered irrational reactions to problems that had not even occurred yet. In the childless past, breakdowns were simply annoyances calculated into travel time, but now they represented danger. The initial "uh oh" from Fritz's lips as he gazed at the dashboard lights used to make my stomach hit my knees, but we were always rescued and were no worse for wear. Yet confidence in a good outcome, like the miraculous way Petey had started years ago, grew shorter in supply. My imagination had us abandoned but never rescued. My mind was unable, in its paralysis, to draw out such a potential predicament to its likely conclusion, a tow truck. On long trips I fixated on impending doom. It was not logical, but logic never wins a fight with fear. And facts don't do any good either.

Finally, in the mid-nineties, we realigned our automobile image when we bought a friend's midnight blue '82 Mercedes 300SD Turbo Diesel for a song. It replaced an '82 Plymouth Gran (not to be confused with "Grand") Fury that—among other cosmetic issues—had lost its soft gray headliner on a junior high Sunday school field trip, leaving the foam rubber of the interior roof exposed with all the little darlings' initials carved into it. This car was just generally worn out and, to put it kindly, ugly as sin, and no Sunday school outing was going to change that. The Fury and the Mercedes were in fact made in the same year, but so were Meg Ryan and I. Driving this dream compared to every other vehicle we'd owned was the difference between being pulled by a Clydesdale and riding a jackass. But like that boy in the country, can you put a man in a Mercedes, without the Mercedes getting into the man?

Fritz proved that he had maintained his generosity when he offered one of his students the use of our Mercedes for the senior banquet. But an ugly panic and possessiveness came over me. The car had come to represent travel security, seldom known to me and worth appearing selfish to protect. We'd readily loaned out our earlier cars to "friends," more a sign of their stupidity than our generosity, but this car actually had worth and had quickly gripped the steering wheel of my heart. But Fritz convinced me my fears were groundless and my better instincts prevailed—until a little after midnight. The phone rang. The boy had bottomed out in a big ditch during a storm and badly bent the undercarriage. So now even the mighty Mercedes was vulnerable.

"Badly bent" was an understatement. The tires rolled from outside to inside like the orbit of Jupiter. The international cast of mechanics who had maintained this very car for its previous two qualified owners shook their heads slowly back and forth as we drove up. The Lebanese shop owner muttered, "My gahd, whadid ya do to dis cah?" We stood in front of these inquisitors exposed for what we really were—luxury car imposters. Everything worked out fine, but one night not long afterwards the status-symbol hood ornament was stolen off the car. I was convinced the mechanics had done it. I could picture them sewing the chrome peace sign on the bib of a frock, coming to our house, and forcing me to wear it in shame to the grocery store until my net worth increased.

The truth was that by the time we owned the Mercedes, after those rapid-succession breakdowns, we had gone a long stretch—years—without any major incidents of our own. When the third boy came along, in an unprecedented move we bought a year-old vehicle that Chrysler had recently invented called a minivan with some money I inherited from my aunt. Still, I remember many trips in the backseat of it (our oldest got carsick and had to sit up front) trying to ignore the whirring noise of the tires on the road by playing my sons' Game Boy. On a trip to Maine, I must have played thirty games of Mario Tennis so I wouldn't imagine a tire blowing or a piston flying out from under the hood. Often my heart palpitated and sank partially to my knees over some noise or Fritz's furrowed brow, a look he always has when he drives but I always misinterpret as a sign of trouble. I had it all right—classic anxiety, sweat and all. Oddly, I was never afraid of accidents even though we regularly traveled one of the most congested stretches of highway in the nation in the left lane the whole way owing to someone's slightly leaded right foot.

My traveling fears eventually moved from the senseless to the debilitating. Although I spent most of my day in the car carting three little boys around town, long-distance highway driving became a man's job. With my breakdown fear and steering wheel capitulation combined, the thought of driving alone on I-95, even to a friend's house only twenty minutes north, sent my heart fluttering again. I obfuscated my terror by turning down invitations to visit people by making up excuses or by rooking friends into going with me. I hid my insanity from my friend Dianne, who twice a year drove blithely alone to Virginia after moving to Massachusetts. She worked for a ministry on Martha's Vineyard and could use any of its cars from the community parking lot, trusting that the maintenance guy had kept it up to speed. She'd hop in an old Volvo or Skylark and drive fourteen hours by herself. Dianne's "bravery" made me feel like an octogenarian who needed a visit from a sprightly young person.

Though I didn't do anything to change, I felt more and more trapped by this irrationality. I knew I had a problem that would eventuate in me becoming just like someone I met twenty years ago in a woman's organization. After giving her directions to something which involved getting on the highway for the distance of one exit, the already dowdy fortyish woman replied, "Oh no. I'm not getting on 64. Tell me another way." To be fair, she may have had an Audi Fox in her past too. But her quick refusal to do something so simple and harmless struck me as more than a little weird. And here I was twenty years later.

The crazy thing about craziness is that it comes to some sort of head. And if you don't deal with it privately, then it may make an unexpected public appearance. I really hoped to avoid that and got a perfect opportunity to make some headway on my highway-itis. My dear college roommate Liane, who lives in Maine, called a couple of Junes ago to say she was coming to a conference in D.C. Could I meet her there for one night? I asked myself, "She's driving sixteen hours, can I drive less than two?" What really made me sad was that instead of excitement at the prospect of an all-too-rare rendezvous with one of my closest friends in the world, I felt a wave of panic. I told Liane I'd get back to her.

For a couple of weeks I mulled it over. This trip would involve not only driving alone, but also finding my way around Washington, a city that is historic in our family for the other car hazard—getting miserably lost. (I still don't know how we made it home from my brother-in-law's rehearsal dinner there.) I'm not sure what the Frenchman L'Enfant was thinking when he designed D.C. with all those blasted traffic circle things that branch off into eight choices. Once you enter the deadly circular zone and impatient drivers start bunching up all around you, it is impossible to read the tiny print on the signs and get in the correct lane.

Still, an inner voice—and a book—told me it was time to face this fear. I had received this book about anxiety from an art client. It was coauthored by his wife. Not my normal choice for reading material, but for some reason I grabbed it on my way out the door to pick up my brother from the airport. While waiting for him I read how an anxious person absolutely must do the thing that makes them the most afraid. That chapter instantly reminded me of my oldest son Cheston who had already figured this out when he was about five or six. He'd been terrified for weeks to venture down the steps alone to the dark basement playroom. Then one morning he found me in my bedroom to tell me something. In that w-dominated, Elmer Fudd-ish voice that I so miss, Cheston pwocwaimed, "Mommy, I am so pwoud of myseuf. I fay-ist my feuwrs and went down to da pwaywoom by mysef." I called Liane to tell her I'd be there around four that Friday and echoed her "I am so excited!" She didn't need to know that I was lying through my chattering teeth.

I got the car completely checked out and made plans to meet three friends for lunch in Ashland, a few miles north and on the way to Washington. During the meal that parachutist's feeling I got in my old Volkswagen came over me in waves. Perhaps these women would want to sit at the restaurant all day discussing some big personal problem. Maybe I'd break a bone on the way out, or get sick. We had a great time, but lunch was clearly over and it was time to go. They had no idea how tense I was at the prospect of driving up Route 95 by myself. And I wasn't about to mention it for an even greater fear that they would look at me like I'd grown instantly dowdy.

Remembering the book, I approached the interchange and faced the challenge. It was as though a voice came breaking through the clouds saying, "Choose ye this day: 95 South, land of home and safety, or 95 North, road to bravery and fun." Setting my jaw and blinking my left turn signal, I pointed the minivan's nose north toward the nation's capital. I may have even dredged up a little Spanky for the occasion: "I don't know where I'm goin' but I'm on my way." That was only partially true since not only did we join AAA, but I wiped them out of all the free maps they carried of Washington D.C. and studied them like they held the key to Blackbeard's treasure. I also had my cell phone, which I checked and rechecked for battery power like Lady Macbeth. It is good to have faith, but it doesn't hurt to be overly prepared for emergencies either.

It took an hour, all the way to Fredericksburg, for the irregular heartbeats and deep breaths to subside and before I actually began to enjoy myself. The one concession I made to my neurosis was turning off the air conditioner when the traffic backed up, like it does every day up there, to cut down on my chances of overheating as I crept over the 14th Street Bridge for an hour. By then I was downright enjoying myself despite the rings of sweat under my arms. I'd listened to part of a book on tape and the traffic gave me some great opportunities for people watching in between checking my gauges like Rusty Wallace.

Pulling into the Hyatt's parking lot in northwest D.C., I couldn't remember a time I felt so good inside. To a stranger, calling a two-hour drive up I-95 an "accomplishment" for a forty-something person would have sounded . . . crazy. But it was a very real accomplishment to me. Liane and I had the greatest time catching up, then met another old friend, Jane, who lives up there, and we all had dinner in a cool Greek restaurant in the hip Adams-Morgan section of town. A bottle of wine between us later, the conversation got very deep and loving, the kind that reeks with trust among old friends. I received and I think was able to pass along some much-needed encouragement that evening. I wouldn't have missed it for the world.

Since then I have made several trips alone, and while I still don't relish it, I can do it. Just writing that now makes me want to point my finger in the mirror and laugh at myself. But I am doing better. Instead of focusing on the means of "loco"-motion—whether pushing, towing, hitchhiking, walking, or even *driving*—I try to remember that we always made it home. Interestingly, the more victory I get over my inner fears by doing the thing that most frightens me, the more confident I am in general. To risk sounding a little like Jesse Jackson, my "trust factor" must outweigh my "what if" factor. It was indeed the "what ifs" that caused those years of worry, and as with most anxieties, they always led to some imaginary, outrageous, untimely demise. But it's clear to me now that there is more than one way to stop living.

it's a dirty job

Give her the fruit of her hands; and let her own works praise her in the gates.

Proverbs 31:31 KJV

I make things for a living. I like the first part, the making—it's the "living" I could live without. Six or eight times a year for the past dozen years of my ever-shortening life, I have packed my heavy, breakable ceramic wares into twenty white banker's boxes and crammed them into my minivan. I then drive with no rear view whatsoever to either a swanky private school, an upscale church, or an open-air venue in a quaint town somewhere in Virginia. The first thing to fall out of the back is the clanky orange and black metal dolly that I bought at a neighbor's yard sale. Back and forth, back and forth I clank, from the car to my ten-by-ten space, thinking about only one thing as the sweat rolls down my back:

"What's that deposit slip going to say at the end of the day?"

At first this backbreaking, financially unpredictable "career" was fun, but the older I have gotten the more I have struggled with how ridiculous it seems and wondered how I got to this point. Slinging mud could not have been more different from how I envisioned my life back in college when I felt like a young history scholar. Nor do I remember any sloshed adult pulling me aside at a graduation cocktail party either and whispering, "I've got one word for you . . . *ceramics*." Like *The Graduate*, I kind of stumbled into my affair with a bag of clay from what seemed at the time like boredom or lack of direction, or more truthfully an aversion to what I'd call real nine-to-five work.

Looking more closely in hindsight, though, it may have been in some plan after all, once I got through trying—yet again—to live somebody else's life because I thought I should have an important-sounding, adult job, one that sends you a fat W-2 form at the end of the year. I have been thoroughly self-employed, but the story of my muddy business, which I proudly named House Afire, won't be written up by Wall Street analysts any time soon. No one would believe it. Besides, those stories are meant to inspire awe at financial prowess, not feats of clay.

Even though I took art every year from eighth through twelfth grades, I considered it a hobby, not a potential profession. That was before motherhood and a summer visit to Nantucket. If one is wired with a good deal of cheapness and not a whole lot of artistic security, never underestimate the inspirational power of shopping. My friend Dianne's sister threatened never to shop with her again because, like me, instead of seeing something and saying, "Oh how beautiful," Dianne's first and sustained reaction—to the point of taking notes—is always, "Oh my gosh, we could make that." In the summer of 1988 that very thought entered my head and changed the direction of my life. We were staying on that quaint Massachusetts island with my husband's whole clan in the little town of Madaket. I was just emerging from those early child-rearing cocoon years, so one morning while everyone went to the beach I ventured blissfully alone into Nantucket Town—just to look.

On a table in the corner of a tiny gallery stood a handmade clay canister set. It was obviously created with someone's fingers, since you could see the pinch marks. In contrast to the gritty, dull, earth-toned, duck motif popular in pottery and everything else in the eighties, this set's shiny, light yellow glaze and hatch-marked texture captivated me. At the intersection of each crisscross was a tiny, pink, hand-formed rosebud. The colors, and especially the pink rose buds, spoke to some ancient force in my spirit that said, "Buy me." The price tag countered with, "Put me down before you break me."

The flour, sugar, coffee, and tea containers stayed in the gallery, but they had thrown down the ceramic gauntlet. Long after we returned from New England, the refrain "I could make that" rang in my head. Little did I know it then, but the memory of that adorable and expensive set was the germ of my business idea, and the only thing on my mind when we returned from vacation was finding a bag of clay. My first thought was to look an hour away outside of Colonial Williamsburg at an unless-you've-been-there-you-wouldn't-believe-it place called the Williamsburg Pottery Factory. It was as though the colonial part of town just had too much good, restrained eighteenth-century taste for the square mileage, so the city planners threw in the Pottery Factory for balance. In town you can buy pewter candlesticks and brass William and Mary trivets, and on the way out you can stock up on crocheted toilet paper cov-

179

ers and miniature adobe houses. Surely I could find a simple bag of clay there. It was the Pottery Factory, after all. After asking three or four clerks who looked at me like I'd asked to see their Ming vases, one veteran pointed me to a corner where a few bags of white clay lay. For a capital investment of five bucks, my business plan began to take shape.

Following my nose, I soon discovered the ceramic underground in my town, including Campbell's, a huge warehouse in an industrial area near the racetrack run by two very kind, laid-back brothers. I then happened upon a storefront shop in a strip mall between a video store and a beauty parlor that would fire my little clay doodads in their kiln for a few dollars each. It was called "Gigi's Porcelains" but owned by Lena. She was a big-haired, buxom woman who always wore nice polyester dresses and bossed around her lanky cowboy-type husband, who seemed to like it. She was so patient while I picked her brain on the many trips I made both to drop off my creations in their highly breakable, dried-out greenware stage and then to retrieve them once they'd been fired safely to what is called bisque. The days in between seemed like an eternity.

That was the pattern I followed, back and forth to Gigi's, until I finally bought my own kiln from a very nice woman whose teeth were so horizontal her lips couldn't cover them all the way. She'd advertised for several weeks in the paper, so I guessed she might be eager to sell for less than the $250 she was asking. One fall Saturday afternoon while Fritz and the three little boys waited in the station wagon, I entered her ranch-style house, where every day was a holiday. Ceramic Santas, Easter bunnies, pumpkins, and leprechauns of all types and sizes greeted me on anything that had a flat surface, including the floor. Moving very carefully around to the laundry room, we came upon the round, white, brick and metal oven that would be the key to my financial future. I executed my well thought-out plan for negotiating the deal.

"I'll give you $175 for it," I blurted, trying not to show my weakness because I really wanted it.

"Well, I was hoping to get more than that . . . but okay."

I almost felt like apologizing but quickly made small talk instead so she wouldn't change her mind. We shoved the new bit of overhead into the car. I had never felt so much power—220 volts to be exact.

My first work space was a half sheet of smooth plywood on a tool bench in a five-by-twelve-foot room off the basement. In the beginning I just played around with the clay and amazingly, like riding a bike, all the principles of hand building came back as though the dozen years after high school had never elapsed. I made a teapot, and then another, and then another. I added some jewelry ideas. (I never did rip off the canister set because trying to attach only three or four of the little rosebuds was enough to drive me nuts.) Before long I had enough inventory to enter a show that a friend held in her home in the nicest section of town.

I'd heard all kinds of things about this informal sale, like that people like me made thousands in only two days. My new group of friends, these veteran creatives, raved on and on about well-heeled ladies who waltzed through the porch, kitchen, and living room waving hundred dollar bills in your face and acting as though they were at a bakery. "I'll take one of those, and one of those, and a dozen of those." The first year I did it, those very same old-timers kept repeating, "I just don't understand where all the people are. Maybe it's the economy." I'd hear the "you should have been here last time" refrain often in my new hobby/business. But during that first winter show standing behind a card table of my wares, I didn't care. It was there in Liz's kitchen that a person first opened up her Gucci wallet and gave me *her* money for something that had originated in *my* mind and found shape through *my* hands. So what if the two days' receipts represented a loss, since they didn't even cover my entry fee. That was the end of my stupid idealism. From then on, I was in it for the dough.

This was the late eighties and the sexiest word of those times, though French, didn't have too much to do with love. Everyone wanted to be an entrepreneur, even if they couldn't spell it. My elementary school–aged kids didn't miss its overuse, asking, "Mommy, what's an onta-panooer?" The term adopted a perverted sense of the artistic—the lone visionary bringing society a message or a "creation" it didn't even know it needed. The other craze that lasted on into the nineties, especially among women, was creating a home business. If you could do both at once, becoming an entrepreneur who ran her business from home—with the stipulation that the business have either "consultant" or "software" in its title—you too could be raking in the cash in your bathrobe.

By stretching the definition, I could have called myself an entrepreneur with a home-based business, but somehow that was a little too sexy for the dirt-based operation in my basement. No lone visionary here. In fact, as the desire to make more money and the need to justify staying at home grew, I subconsciously exploited my previously innocent artistic expression and began to make things out of fear, things based on what I thought the customer wanted. Most of my work ended up being commissions for pins of kids, or family caricatures in clay cutouts, or someone's home etched and painted on a piece of flat clay or done in a three-dimensional, architectural replica.

When my suppliers (Gigi's, aka Lena) went out of business, I was in a panic to find the paints that had become as familiar to me as my own children. Fern,

Everglade, and Forest Green together created shaded foliage. Indian Red was perfect for bricks, Fiesta Turquoise for sky, and Charcoal Gray for roofs. I found them at what would become a very familiar haunt in a pretty unfamiliar part of town. Without its hand-painted, blue, block-lettered sign—"CERAMIC SHOW-CASE"—across the top of a low white stucco building between a transmission service and a used car lot, my newfound supplier would have been easy to miss. It was run by Myrtle and Ralph and their daughter Julie, entrepreneurs all. Myrtle was a round, pleasant woman with a curly gray perm who mostly sat in a back room watching soap operas and painting. I could see her back there through the shelves of merchandise, most of which made the Pottery Factory look like Tiffany's. But this was what set Ceramic Showcase apart from other shops: row after row of ready-to-paint greenware made from plaster molds.

It was Ralph's job to pour all the molds and keep the shelves stocked. He was tall, lean, and stone deaf. He wore an old gas station shirt with a name patch that said Frank on it, which tripped me up every time I tried to be friendly. His navy blue work pants were always covered in dust, and for some reason, maybe from a lifetime of trying not to drop the brittle greenware, he never lifted his feet when he walked. You could hear him shuffling along the gritty, worn wood floor like a zombie. I wondered sometimes what would happen if I rubbed his head, picturing an atomic cloud of clay dust rising above him.

Julie told me that the small back room was stacked to the ceiling with 7,000 molds. I believed her. This was the place you went to find those Easter bunnies, Santas, leprechauns, and Blessed Mothers to sit on your lawn, if you were so inclined. They also had adorable, tasteful miniature tea sets, beautiful angels, and huge bowls and platters to paint how you wanted for as little as $4 and no more than $10. Among those dark, narrow rows of cinder block and plywood shelves beckoned paint-your-own Elvis planters, life-sized kitty-cat lamps, and, believe it or not, about at eye level, a coffee mug in the shape of a female breast.

Even after just a few hundred dollars of a self-made clay fortune, I was hooked on being my own boss and committed to staying at home with the boys while they were still young. But I realized just how little inventory I could actually produce with my own two hands. Once Fritz got the idea of doing a college building in relief, we began reproducing them the same way Ralph did, using a mold. The Campbell brothers even came over to our house to show us how to make a simple box mold. I made the original in three levels of clay and placed it in a plywood box with sides held together by huge clamps. We then poured about three gallons of milky-looking plaster into the box on top of my original and let it harden for fifteen minutes (in which time it gets fascinatingly hot) before releasing the clamps and popping off those wooden sides. Once we flipped it over and extracted my original master, we had what Marx called our very own "means of production"—only at first we looked more like the Marx brothers. It took us six or eight pourings to figure out that we had to seal the seams of the clamped box. The process wasn't so fascinating when hot, milky plaster started furiously draining out all sides of the box and hardening on the floor. In those attempts, the procedure included the heretofore unmentioned steps of cussing and wall banging. Once we got the plaster mold thing down, I remembered Ralph and Myrtle. Every so often, in "what in the world am I doing with my life" moments, I'd imagine us in the future—Fritz shuffling through our basement carrying a greenware Nefertiti and me with a curly gray perm painting a bunny with *All My Children* blaring in the background.

After we heard that it would be a good idea to have a mold of a mold since you lose the detail on your piece as the plaster wears out, we found a chemical substance that we dubbed "flubber." The idea was to mix this rubbery goo, which resembled lime Jell-O left in the back of the refrigerator for a month, and pour it, instead of liquid plaster, into a plaster mold to make a permanent master piece. It was wildly expensive and uncooperative. When I walked in on Fritz wrestling with a blob of flubber as little balls of it covered the basement playroom floor, it was clear we needed a better research and development department. I had also come up with a teapot design of a dog that made me wonder, after making a dozen or so by hand, how to make a mold of something three-dimensional. Right when we really needed an expert, we found C. J.—only like others in this "profession," that wasn't his real name, but in this case the name confusion went beyond quirkiness.

C. J. was new in town and had come into Ceramics Showcase offering his mold-making services. He also had a job grooming dogs at Pet World. Myrtle passed this on to me, and when I called the pet store, I could have sworn he told me his name was C. J. Jones, although there was a lot of barking in the background. So when at the end of the conversation he said he was C. J. Johnson, I took it as my mistake. When he asked to be paid in cash since his checking account wasn't set up because his license hadn't been renewed because the DMV in California had been negligent, I was too ecstatic that I'd found a mold-man to care how flimsy this sounded.

C. J. was kind of a know-it-all, but since we were know-nothings, we made a good match. Overall he was a very pleasant guy, in his early fifties, tall with a big belly and a decent comb-over. He insisted on coming to our house to make the doggie teapot mold. His expertise came from many years of working at a commercial ceramics plant out West. When we got to know him better, we asked what brought him all the way across the country. "Well, my wife died tragically in a car accident, and I just couldn't take the memories. My nineteen-year-old son and I just packed up and left." This sad story engendered a lot of pity in us, and C. J. began to speak of his wife often on his consultation visits. Besides all the personal sharing, he delivered the goods. He also showed Fritz the foolproof way to mix and "de-gas" the plaster ("get your hands down in there, boy, and mix it up") so every batch was perfect, a skill we have used over and over.

Now that I had C. J. in place, it was easy to think up more teapots and get him to make the molds. It was too good to be true. He made two dogs, a mermaid, and a little bird for me. He even groomed our dog Mabel. But after a year or so, it became harder to reach him. I had taken him a master of a horse/cowboy boot teapot weeks earlier but could not get in touch to find out if he'd done it and how I could get it. Finally one late winter afternoon he called, sounding out of breath. He said he'd be over around 8:30 that night with the teapot and his son. I was to have the $150 cash ready for him. No cash, no whimsical horse mold. Something in his voice tripped a long-overdue warning bell, and I finally got the creeps, especially since Fritz was out of town on a business trip. After all the times I had already been alone with the guy, I now felt threatened and called my seventy-year-old neighbor Andy to come over.

After that mysterious nighttime visit, C. J. disappeared. Since he never did have a home number, I tried calling another shop owned by sisters who smoked like chimneys, the place he ended up making the molds.

They hadn't seen him in weeks. Then one day as Ceramic Showcase's door opener ding-donged when I walked in, my eyes met a sign hanging off the counter. Instead of the usual notice of firing prices, there hung an FBI "Wanted" poster, strange enough for a hobby store, but absolutely shocking when it turned out to be a mug shot . . . of C. J.! Frozen in my tracks, I was afraid to look closely. But really, what could he have done? Made counterfeit Snow Babies or Mickey Mouse statuettes? Reading the fine print, I saw that he and his son were fugitives from California, wanted on several counts of car theft and, to my horror as I thought back on all the times he was in our house, child molestation.

I got a grip on my facial expression and asked Julie what she knew. She said an agent had come into Showcase, and all the other clay joints in town, looking for him. The FBI knew he was here and would most likely look for work in the ceramics network. I could not say a word because of the shock, but was thinking how in an innocent attempt to automate our home business, Fritz and I had aided and abetted a really bad criminal. I felt a bit faint and left with my six jars of Fern Green paint without confessing to knowing anything about this C. J. person.

As it turned out, the feds tracked C. J. down at Pet World. I could just envision the scene. He would be in a back room with a Lhasa apso on the table, about to clip its nails or do some ungodly dog thing to it, as guys in navy blue FBI jackets went slinking past parakeets and salamanders with their guns drawn. The agents would yell "Freeze!" and dogs would bark, hamsters would wheel in fright, and cockatiels would squawk like Jimmy Cagney, "You're going to the Big House. You're going to the Big House. Ye-ah, shee."

Now what should I do? Are the teapot molds and their issue ill-gotten gains and tainted goods? I did profit from someone concealing the truth, but so did lots of people on Wall Street in those days. The hard fact is that before he got sent up, C. J. was the turning point in our home-based business. When we met him we had two molds. Now, based on his advice, Fritz has made over twenty-five flat ones, and we're still cranking out teapots from the molds he made for us. Even though I still paint almost every single piece, having a production scheme, however homegrown, has made all the difference in output.

After seeing the term on a tax form, I've taken to calling myself a "manufacturer." Manufacturer carries so much less baggage than "artist," plus I like the industrial sound to it as much as I love the industrial areas of town I visit for my supplies. Calling myself a manufacturer makes me feel legitimate. I know this doesn't square with the starving artist ideal, but having bread-and-butter items makes it less scary than depending completely on those pieces that come directly from my imagination. However, there is no comparison in the professional satisfaction department. When someone buys my reliefs, I am happy for the money, but when a stranger walks up and "gets" my woman-trapped-in-a-sofa lamp, then gets it with her Visa card, I am genuinely excited about more than just the dough. It's the communication, the essence of creativity, that matters then. I still take her credit card, or cash, or check.

Even with the warm fuzzies, everything about the business climate of the nineties pressured me to "go national," as a friend's mother put it, with some of my things. Well-meaning but generally uncreative people readily advised me how "if you could just do (fill in the blank—lighthouses, kitty cats, Elvises) . . . you could make a killing." No matter that I really don't care for cats and it was all I could do to generate income and inventory from what was already in place. What onlook-

188

ers seemed to think was all-important was not what I was actually doing in the basement, but how close I was to making it to some ceramic big time, like becoming a dust-covered Martha Stewart. This was the true entrepreneur's presupposition of success. And they were often still my presuppositions, too. Attempts to get "there" led to wholesale dead ends and retail disappointments, including one with a patient and kind couple named the Yees (his first name was Gee). They ran a small ceramic manufacturing business that I first visited in their home, a tri-level overrun with cats and plaster molds and their combined smells. Once the Yees moved into a big warehouse we almost had a match, but my things ultimately just didn't look like my things. That is the problem with selling real, tangible goods. Even though I called most of my work "manufactured," it still had a whole lot of me in it. But if I ever do find a place that can do it right and cheap, artistic integrity will be just a philosophical concept.

So I carry on, filling orders for flat house tiles and three-dimensional replicas and painting my reliefs while yelling out the answers to the questions on *Jeopardy!* Then, mostly in the fall, it's time for the dog and pony and mermaid and birdie show again. The most recent show (a nonartist's term for "sale") was in Williamsburg, right on Duke of Gloucester Street. I had spent many days as an idealistic, analytical history student walking this very street with friends, discussing religion and politics. Not today. There were price tags to stick and my own kid to send to college. Back then I never would have thought that one day's trip to the Williamsburg Pottery Factory for a bag of clay would be more influential to my life's path than my four years at William and Mary.

If my business were charted like the Dow Jones Industrial Average, then the previous year's Williamsburg show would have been a Space Needle spike. People had filed into my booth like angels at the Pearly Gates. I could not wrap the pieces and cock the portable Visa contraption fast enough. It looked more like the deli counter than an art show, and I was tempted to hand out little paper numbers. After all those years, all those hours spent reading a book at a "sale," finally, finally I could later describe *my* day—not the day of the person next to me—using that rare but glorious term, "hotcakes."

So naturally I was excited when a year rolled around and the October Williamsburg sale came again. The show began at 10:00 A.M. and by 10:30 I realized what an exception last year had been. The familiar consolations began in my head: "At least it didn't rain," " I hope I at least make my $100 entry fee," "At least the lady with the jewelry is selling." Just then a couple I knew from home walked by. He is a history professor, and they had been at the Williamsburg Inn for a conference on subjects I used to know a lot about. His wife asked if it were hurtful when people walked by without buying or even stopping. Hurtful was an interesting interpretation. Her question hearkened back to the notion that my "profession" was really some kind of sadomasochistic love affair I'd fallen into an ego ago. Perhaps to avoid having an emotional breakdown in front of them, I read one of my new greeting cards. My voice broke into a sustained giggle and the wife teased me, "Look at you, laughing at your own stuff." Considering the morning, I said, "Somebody has to."

The crowds picked up after noon. Before long it was business as usual—mothers yanking kids away from my breakable things, big men asking, "So you actually have a kiln," and everyone trying to wiggle the tops back onto my teapots. Then what could have been a ten-year-old me walked up. She outstretched her chubby arms, swinging her patent leather pocketbook, opened wide her brown eyes, and dramatically pronounced, "This stuff is *adorable!* My mom would love this, and this, and this. It is so *adorable!*" Of course I instantly liked this little girl and we had a nice chat. Later an elderly man, at least eighty, walked up during a lull and said, "You must have fun doing this, but I wouldn't want to live in your brain."

The brown-eyed girl and the old man reminded me why I kept subjecting myself to this setup. It was a reminder I needed often ever since those early days at Liz's house when the wife of a real painter said to me in an ominous tone, "You can't do the art life halfway. It has to be an all-out commitment." She had supported her husband's work for years, and I was new at this life. She kindly fell short of using the word "sacrifice." Yes, I was a home-based entrepreneur, running a business in an explosively prosperous time. But over and over I have had to accept the fact that the story of House Afire wasn't going to be featured on CNBC any time soon. I'll never be able, despite my longstanding desire, to use the word "parlay," as in "she parlayed a bucket of mud into a multimillion dollar a year operation" in the introduction to a corporate coffee table book.

The truth is, as my mother is fond of saying, "people do what they want to do." She's right. I have followed the yellow ceramic road because, despite the ridiculous byways and frustrating detours, I have walked it by myself and have not been driven by someone else. I have to believe my business plan was also part of the bigger plan for my life, designed by one that knows the real me. The story of House Afire has been a trip for sure, a seek-and-ye-shall-find journey of the most absurd order. The fact that I've had no AAA TripTik either has made the journey even more dependent on the kindness of friends and strangers (some very strange) and a lot of grace to keep going. I'll never forget one spring day about five years in when it hit me that I had absolutely no work lined up. *Well, this is it,* I thought. *Get out the classifieds.* The next day the phone rang and rang. When I went to bed, I had eight commissions.

If creativity really is love, then it needs to be blind. Riding home from that show in Williamsburg, thoughts comparing the receipts from all the months of tedious work with what many people casually bring home every single week started to tempt me toward infidelity. Stories of easy money filled the air then. It was difficult in those days not to feel like you were the only loser left in America still selling things that could be put in a shopping bag. But as seductive as corporate and cyber worlds appeared, I would have missed the earthier pleasures I have come to take for granted.

You haven't lived until you've slid your arms down into a bucket of slip, or liquified mud, up to the elbows, then felt its cool moisture dry to form dirt evening gloves. Watching a stock ticker couldn't match watching that same velvety brown slip pour into a plaster mold and magically turn into a teapot. No IPO could rival opening the kiln after the final firing, when the piece is shiny and in full color. And while art is a solitary pursuit, I've had colleagues. They are the other artists I've grown to love over years and years of sharing our lives during slow shows to the point we resented it when a customer finally did come and interrupted our stories. And for me, rather than seeing the world divided into eighth- and sixteenth-shares, it's been good to experience the world in Fiesta Turquoise, Santa Fe Sunset, Petal Pink, and my old friend Fern Green.

Only fools fall in love. That one hundred square feet of booth and my studio at home hold the tangible results of a very intimate process between my imagination and my hands. Suffocation, ridiculousness, and occasional resentment aside, I don't think I could live without that intimacy.